Condoms and Hot Tubs Don't Mix

An Anthology of AWKWARD SEXCAPADES

Edited by
Jennie Jarvis and Leslie Salas

Published 2018 by Beating Windward Press LLC

For contact information, please visit:
www.BeatingWindward.com

Copyright © Beating Windward Press LLC, 2018

All Rights Reserved
Book Design by Priscila Santa Rosa, 2018
Cover Illustration by BABS! the great, 2018

First Edition
ISBN: 978-1-940761-38-1

All rights reserved. No part of this publication may be reproduced or transmitted in any other form or for any means, electronic or mechanical, including photocopy, recording or any information storage system, without written permission of the copyright holder.

Table of Contents

Foreword 1
    Jennie Jarvis and Leslie Salas
Why I Hate the Title of this Book 5
    Matt Peters

We Broke the Dictionary 21
    Stacey Balkun
Dimanche Gras 2009 23
    Missy Wilkinson
Clippity-Clop What-Not 31
    Steve Meador
Anything but Boredom 35
    Cecilia Fernandez
Love in the Dark 41
    BABS! the great
Demon Penis Octopus 43
    Bethany DuVall
The Lay At Gay Days 61
    Jameson Tabard
Having 69
    Timothy DeLizza
A Natural Desire 79
    BABS! the great

Watching Porn With My Mother 81
  Peter M. Gordon
Paper Cranes 83
  Alex Celine
The Silver Bullet 97
  Joseph Sheldon
Philosophy and Fugue 101
  Holly Elliott
Love in the Time of Collies 103
  Lisa Lanser Rose
The Killer Whales 109
  Leah Mueller
Pretty in Plastic 115
  Catherine Carson
Dress up Night 119
  BABS! the great
Laid Over 121
  G.B. Lindsey
Play Through the Pain 129
  C.C. Reed
Francisco 133
  Gemma Cooper-Novack
Getting Lewd on Ludes 137
  Jim Ross
Love is in the Air 159
  BABS! the great
What You Finally Attend To 161
  Chelsey Clammer
Another Friday Night With Mr. Fun 167
  John King

Penis Cheese 177
    Heather Startup
Coptus Interuptus 187
    BABS! the great
Ants 189
    Anusha V.R.
Hard Workers 191
    Kate Rigby
Boy In the Bathroom 197
    Nina Robins
The Penis Fly Trap 199
    Anne Champion

Editors Bios 217
Contributor Bios 219
Awkward Sex Fact Citations 231

Foreword
by Jennie Jarvis and Leslie Salas

He took her into his arms. "Darling," he crooned. "I can't live without you."

She tried to push him away. "We can't," she cried. "Not until we've proclaimed our vows."

Her delicate fingers slipped down the glistening rounds of his perfectly chiseled chest. She couldn't help but notice his washboard abs flexing and those delicious biceps bulging as he gripped her waist. She felt her cheeks warm to red. Her soft pinkness moistened.

He pulled her closer.

Against her leg, she felt his thick, quivering member pressing through the fabric of his slacks.

"I must have you," he said, and pressed his Cupid's bow lips firmly against hers.

"No," she mumbled, but her body betrayed her words.

He gently threw her onto the soft, feather bed. Her generous bosom heaved with each anticipatory breath.

As he lowered himself on top of her, his manpurse swayed gently, as his passion --

Stop. What the hell is that?

What? It's a sex scene.

"His manpurse swayed gently"?

Would you rather I called them his balls?

It's better than "manpurse".

I was being poetic.

But you aren't being real. Real consensual sex isn't overly coercive and falsely romantic like that.

Yeah, but they say you can't write about sex like it really is.

Why not?

Sex in real life is awkward and messy.

And weird and silly and cringeworthy.

Sex is trying out the Kama Sutra and failing miserably.

Sex is having a lover go down on you, and then having your pubic hair ripped out when it gets stuck in their braces.

Sex is spending your whole childhood thinking a guy's genitals look like a fig leaf, only to have a rude awakening when you become sexually active.

Sex is trying out a vibrator and having your parents walk in.

Sex is discovering you have a latex allergy the same day you lose your virginity.

Oh, God. That happened to you?

Yeah.

I'm so sorry.

Can we not talk about it anymore? My lady bits hurt just remembering it.

Where were we? Sex is messy and awkward and sloppy and real. It's not all quivering members and moist ladybits and swaying manpurses.

Yeah, and you don't really see that kind of honest sex scene a lot in books.

We're doing our part to help change that.

Let's normalize awkward, realistic sex.

Let's make it literary and poetic.

And raise money for a great cause in the process.

Yes, because who knows the consequences of awkward sex better than Planned Parenthood?

We put the call for submissions out there.

And oh, did our contributors deliver.

Condoms & Hot Tubs is an anthology of stories, essays, and poems that revolve around the awkwardness of sex. Sometimes, it's funny. Sometimes, it's heart-crushing.

But all the times, it's real.

We hope you enjoy.

Jennie Jarvis　　　　Leslie Salas
Co-Editor　　　　　Co-Editor

Why I Hate the Title of This Book
by Matt Peters

Jennie Jarvis left me a voicemail asking if I'd be willing to, and interested in, publishing an anthology of "awkward sex stories" she and Leslie Salas were plotting.

Interested? Sure, I enjoy reading and learning about sex (as sexually themed fiction, full-blown erotica, sex-work memoir, or an anthropological and sociological subject). Willing to publish it? Not so much. I don't have a problem publishing sexual or sexually explicit content; it wasn't the "sex" part that made me hesitate. It was the "anthology" part that made the publisher in me flinch.

"So, a collection of stories about trying to have sex in awkward places or positions?" I asked when we met up for lunch at the campus sports bar & grill. "Like in elevators and canoes and such?"

"No, no, no," Leslie said. "Real sex. Not the perfect, romantic sex people have in books. Or the sweat drenched passionate sex in movies. Actual sex - when the orgasms don't sync up or you're doing something just because your partner enjoys it. Trying out a sex toy for the first time or finally hooking up with someone you've lusted after, but then not being able to get it up or get wet."

"And sex gone wrong," Jennie added. "When the awkwardness of what could be destroys what could have been. When people get in the way of their own happy ending."

Not the usual conversation for a Wednesday lunch at the campus sports bar, but I'd known them for a few years and neither were prudes. And for some reason, I've always been one-of-the-girls when it comes to frank discussions about sex.

"Oh, I get it," I said. "Like how condoms and hot tubs don't mix, right?"

They didn't respond and I figured I'd somehow put my foot in my mouth.

They glanced at each other, and then looked back at me. "Explain," they demanded.

•••

I hit puberty during the United States' AIDS/HIV epidemic of the 1980s. The topic of sexually transmitted diseases and safe sex saturated my teen life. The news reported the spread and rising death count. The gossip papers proclaimed who had HIV or who had secretly died from AIDS. Commercials advertised condoms or raised awareness of sexually transmitted diseases and safe sex. Comedians built routines around AIDS, musicians wrote songs about safe sex, and the radio aired them. People took to the street protesting for and against the rights of infected victims. People also protested for and against sex education and condoms in public schools.

Condoms and Hot Tubs Don't Mix

Beginning in middle school, gym teachers educated us each about safe sex, and I am proud to say I could put a condom on a banana in 4.2 seconds. After all, Ryan White, the AIDS "poster child" was only a year and a half older than me. By the time I finally had sex, my girlfriend and I sure as hell knew we needed protection.

Despite all this, the ever-present anxiety of catching AIDS never ruined the romance or passion of sex. Putting on a condom was just another step in the sex-process. Instead of kiss, grind, take clothes off, kiss, have sex, it was kiss, grind, take clothes off, put condom on, kiss, have sex, throw condom away.

So when my girlfriend's parents went out of town, and we headed for their hot tub, I put on a condom. Safe sex above all. It was only the third time we'd had sex, but doing it in a hot tub was one of those exotic, passionate things we'd seen in movies and TV shows. We were sure it would be sexy and romantic and exciting and adventurous and somehow make the sex better. Maybe she would even enjoy it this time.

The first problem we encountered was that hot tubs are not designed for fucking. They are meant to be sat or reclined in. They aren't deep with smooth sides like pools, or even bathtubs. Three sides and each corner of this hot tub had individual, contoured, bucket seats and the fourth side had a wave-shaped lounger.

This drastically limited our sexual positions. The bucket seats were so deep they didn't allow for a reclined missionary position; my back couldn't bend far enough backwards to get my penis inside her. And switching to more of a lap-dance position was ruined by the hard plastic of the seats next to us smacking her knees and cracking her shins.

We tried the lounger, but again missionary was out, and the only way the lap-dance and cowgirl positions would work was if she was missing a leg. The only flat surface was the floor - two or three square feet in the center where everyone's feet were supposed to go - but that was too deep for us to sit without drowning. A standing doggy style was out because she felt it was too impersonal and disrespectful. (Remember, we were teenagers...)

The solution we found was to ignore the way we were supposed to sit in the hot tub. So we ended up laying across the lounger's lowest part in the missionary position with her head resting (banging) on the edge of the hot tub.

Finally, we could have exotic, passionate, romantic, exciting and adventurous movie sex.

But alas, the laws of hydrodynamics weren't on our side.

Although we got slick and slippery when wet, human skin actually contracts and puckers to give us traction. Well, no, not all the skin. Just the skin we use to grip stuff, which is why fingers and toes wrinkle in the bath.

Water may be slippery, but water is a very poor lubricant. Water's viscosity is low compared to most fluids considered lubricants. So when it fails, there is contact between the moving parts. And this causes friction.

Not to mention the fact that water is a solvent that actually washes away the vagina's natural lubrication. And this causes more friction.

To top it all off, hot water, along with the chemicals used to keep hot tubs crystal clear, ruin a condom's durability. As the condom breaks down, its surface cracks and frays before breaking, making the smooth, slick surface rough. Yup, more friction.

So by the time we'd figured out the fuck-shui for hot tubs and worked into a rhythm, she was complaining, "It hurts."

I slowed down, but didn't stop completely or anything. "It'll be OK," I told her, disappointed that it was happening again.

I took her virginity two weeks earlier. So, while it was our third time having sex together, it was also only the third time she'd had sex ever. The first two times had been painful and uncomfortable for her. I'd hoped the super-awesome-specialness of Hot Tub Sex, and the relaxing properties of hot tubs in general, would help her enjoy it this time. But no.

"It really hurts."

"It'll be OK," I told her again. "I'll make it quick," I added, thinking I'd be as slow and gentle as I could until I came. (Because I still thought sex ended when the man [boy?] ejaculated.)

"No. Stop," she said pushing my chest. "It burns."

I backed away so she could sit up. "Burns?"

She nodded and cupped her hands over her vagina and held it like she'd been kicked there. "Oh, god yes. It really fucking hurts."

Concern and empathy flushed the lust out of my brain, and I considered the problem for a second. "Not like before?"

She shook her head and said, "It stings. Burns. Like a strawberry or road-rash."

A different pain. And we weren't in a bed this time. Maybe it wasn't my chaotic thrusting and gyrating this time.

She was in pain, and I had a puzzle to solve. The sex was over.

We were in the hot tub, in water, so there shouldn't have been any friction to cause a stinging burning strawberry type abrasion. The condom. Condoms are made out of rubber. Tires are also made out of rubber to grip the road, especially wet roads.

"The condom," I said, taking hold of my penis. I tried to slide my hand along the condom, but the condom stuck to my hand. I wasn't gripping it tightly; the condom itself was sticky- almost gummy. "Oh, my god. I'm so sorry," I told her. "I didn't know."

Her labia were red and raw and sore to the touch. She told me later that her vagina had little blisters and abrasions in it. We stuck to foreplay for the next few weeks to work our way back up to actual intercourse.

After a year or so, we had sex in water again, a pool this time, but decided it was safer to avoid practicing safe sex. We'd been together for a long time. She was on the pill. And pools have much better fuck-shui.

•••

Jennie and Leslie's smiles were broad and sinister.

"Exactly like that," Leslie said, laughing.

"You know," Jennie agreed, adding, "I think we found a title."

"Condoms and Hot Tubs Don't' Mix?" Leslie asked.

"Yes."

"No," I said.

"Totally."

Sigh...

•••

So, I understood the type of Awkward Sex stories they wanted to publish, but I still didn't want to publish another anthology.

The first anthology of stories Beating Windward Press published was *The Snuff Syndicate*, a collection of serial killer stories that was complete and ready to go to press when another publisher called it quits. It came to me through an editor friend on a silver platter wrapped with a bow. The writers were to be paid $0.05 a word for their stories and then 100% of the royalties would go to the press. All I had to do was layout the interior of the book and have a cover designed. It was a fun book and a great project, but *The Snuff Syndicate* had come out four years before this lunch with Jennie and Leslie, and I still hadn't made back the money I'd paid out for the stories. Because the writers had been paid upfront, there was no financial incentive for them to promote the book after the initial release.

The second anthology Beating Windward Press tried to publish was never finished. A pair of editors wanted to do a collection about the strange unique jobs writers/artists have taken on to pay their bills while they work on their art. I didn't have time to edit the anthology because I had a day job to pay the bills, but the editors promised to do all the work and hand me a complete and finished manuscript. They wrote up a call for submissions and I posted it on the submission page of Beating Windward's website. I set up an e-mail account for submissions and we all spread the word. We received a lot of great stories and sent out contracts to the writers of the stories we accepted. But then the project fell apart. One had gotten a promotion at her day job and was going through a divorce. The other received a number of better paying writing projects that always came first. No hard feelings. I totally understood. But I was too busy with my full-time job and own personal drama to take over for them.

For the next year or so, the writers selected to be in the anthology checked in on the status of it. Most still believed in the concept and wanted to see it come to life. Some wanted to publish their pieces elsewhere. I didn't want to cancel the anthology, but hated keeping them on the hook and knew I was never going to get to it myself. So, feeling like a failure who couldn't follow through on my grand ideas, I canceled the anthology.

Those were my reasons for not wanting to publish the anthology suggested by Jennie and Leslie. It wasn't that the concept was a bad one, or that I had any objection to sexual content. The press couldn't afford to lose that kind of money again. And I didn't want to feel like a failure again. I had enough to do on my own for the next year or so and it was easier to say no than try and figure out how to make it happen.

But Jennie Jarvis does not accept no for an answer. (Have you seen this woman run a writing conference?) And the condom and hot tub story had convinced her I was the publisher for this book.

"What if you didn't have to actually pay the writers?" she asked.

"Writers need to be paid," I said. "If we don't pay, we won't get good work."

"What if instead of paying them," she asked, "we donated the royalties to charity?"

I'd donated a portion of profits from another book to charity; Beating Windward gives $1 to the New Orleans Area Habitat for Humanity for each copy of *The Parish: An AmeriCorps Story* we sell.

So this idea, I could get behind. "Like what?"

"Something like AIDS United, Advocates for Youth, or Planned Parenthood." Leslie suggested.

"Planned Parenthood," Jennie asserted. "Absolutely."

This was a time when the political atmosphere bubbled with labeling Planned Parenthood as a "baby killing" institution – ignoring the amazing work they do to provide quality healthcare to over two million people across the country and the incredible job they do to promote sexual education and safe sex practices.

"Planned Parenthood," I agreed. "If you can get the writers to agree to that instead of payment, and get a quality collection, I'll publish what you put together."

•••

I didn't agree to support Planned Parenthood for good publicity or bad publicity or because of political allegiances. And not because I'm pro-abortion or I hate children. Abortion had nothing to do with my decision. Planned Parenthood had helped me out once, and I wanted to give back. (Just because I'm male doesn't mean Planned Parenthood doesn't offer any services for me.)

A year or so after the Hot Tub Incident, that girlfriend found out I'd cheated on her, and the only way she would stay with me, and even consider ever having sex with me again, was if I was tested for STDs.

I didn't mind getting tested. I was straight and usually had safe-sex, so I wasn't worried I had an STD. But I was 19, had no medical insurance or even a regular doctor. I was a dishwasher at T.G.I. Fridays making $4.25 an hour and living paycheck to paycheck. Alienated from my parents, I didn't live at home and rented a room from a stranger. I was one of those people who went to the Emergency Room if I had a cold for longer than a week, or, Zarquon forbid, I got in a bicycle wreck. I wasn't even in college, so there was no campus clinic I could go to for an STD test.

I tried to get an STD test at the county health clinic, but without any symptoms I was last on the waiting list for the once-a-month testing they offered. However, at the time, the local Planned Parenthood offered STD testing on a sliding price scale based on income for those without health insurance. Because I was a dishwasher making minimum wage, I got the test for $10.

Planned Parenthood offered services such as birth control, cancer screenings, sex education, fertility testing and treatment, HIV testing and medication, pelvic exams, assistance with sexual dysfunction, STD testing and treatment, pregnancy testing, and other pregnancy-related services. And it offered a non-judgmental facility for the LGBT community to obtain high-quality health care, including hormone therapy for transgender patients.

This was 1993. The internet existed, but I didn't know anyone who used it or had access to it. It didn't even cross my mind to research what was involved with STD tests. The only preparation I did was to shower before my appointment. My girlfriend drove me to the Planned Parenthood clinic and waited until my test was done - to make sure I really did it.

Before the physical testing, a nurse took me to an interview room to assess my STD Risk Factors. I hadn't expected that, but I was straight, so I wasn't too worried about my risk factors.

I was ready for the first few questions because of all the AIDS-Ed I'd had...

Have you ever had sex (vaginal, oral, or anal)?
"Yes."
Have you had more than one sex partner within the past six months?
"Yes." *That's why I'm here...*
When with new or non-steady partners, do you use a condom or barrier?
"Yes." *...usually.*

But then the questions got specific, detailed, and uncensored...

Does your sexual partner have other sexual partners?
"Uhm, not my regular one." *But the girl I cheated on my girlfriend with does.*
Have you had unprotected vaginal sex with more than one partner in the last year?
"No."
Have you had unprotected oral sex with more than one partner in the last year?
"...yes."
Have you ever engaged in sexual behavior with anyone who has many sexual partners?
"...yes."
Have you been forced to have oral, vaginal or anal sex (against your will)?

"No."

Have you ever had sex with someone who has been forced to have oral, vaginal or anal sex?

> "Oh, uhm, yes." *Two of my sexual partners had been molested as children. And the girl I lost my virginity to had been raped before.*

Are you bisexual?

> "No."

Have you ever had sex with someone who is bisexual?

> "...yes." *One of my sexual partners was bisexual and had been in a relationship with a bisexual guy before me.*

Have you ever had oral-genital or anal sexual contact with a male?

> "No."

Have you ever had your penis in a male's mouth (receptive oral sex)?

> "No."

Have you ever had a male's penis in your mouth (performed oral sex on a male)?

> "No."

Have you ever used recreational drugs?

> *What the Fuck...* "Yes."

In the past six months, have you had sex with anyone who ever used recreational drugs?

> "Yes."

Have you ever used a needle to inject drugs (not prescribed by a healthcare provider)?

> *Oh, I see where she is going now...* "No."

Have you had sex with someone who ever injected recreational drugs?

> "...yes." *That bisexual side chick had also done heroin a few times.*

Have you ever exchanged drugs or money for sex?
"No."

Have you ever engaged in sexual behavior with anyone who has traded sex for drugs?

> Damn... "...yes." *Again, my bisexual, drug-shooting side chick.*

Have you experienced any form of blood-to-blood or blood-to-body fluid contact?

> *What the fuck... but that makes sense.* "...yes." *I had a few Blood Brothers from when I was a kid. And in more recent years, had "played" vampire a few times, which basically involved bleeding ourselves or each other and drinking each other's blood.*
>
> *Holy shit... I might not "pass" this test.*

•••

These straight forward, in-depth questions laid out exactly how at risk I actually was. And showed me that all the "education" I'd endured during school was an abbreviated, sanitized version of the actual info it would have been nice to have. I mean, I'd heard that I was basically sleeping with everyone that anyone I slept with had slept with before, but that concept didn't really capture the actual scale of those connections. But the nurse at Planned Parenthood didn't have to worry about overstepping any appropriate boundaries or pissing off parents or shocking and offending religious and community leaders. She was there to help me, not placate everyone.

Oh, she was also there to shove a six-inch long cotton swab up my penis.

For the actual testing, the nurse drew my blood to test for HIV/AIDS, syphilis and hepatitis. Then asked me to take my pants off so she could examine my penis. Now, I'd mentally prepared myself to provide answers to personal, embarrassing questions about my sex life in front of a stranger, but didn't have any idea that I was going to stand in front of said stranger with my pants down while she stared at my dick and balls. I assumed everything would be done with a blood or urine test.

The nurse raked a tongue depressor through my pubic hair, checking for crab-lice. I hoped that was it, but then she lifted my penis to look at the underside and rolled my testicles around to examine my scrotum, checking for genital warts and herpes outbreaks. Still not done, she held up a six-inch wooden kabob with a puff of cotton at the end and explained she was going to test for gonorrhea and chlamydia. And to do that, she needed to insert the cotton swab into my penis to obtain a culture. She promised to be gentle. I took a deep breath and clinched my entire body. But then she only inserted the swab three-fourths of an inch into the tip of the penis.

I'd gone in there for a free STD test, but ended up getting a valuable education. A week later I went back and learned I'd passed all the tests and didn't have any sexually transmitted diseases.

So, yes, I support Planned Parenthood. And if Jennie and Leslie could get their writers to donate their royalties, I'd publish their collection.

But I'd have to talk them out of that Condoms and Hot Tubs title.

•••

It's a shame I failed.

We Broke the Dictionary
by Stacey Balkun

You lug
the old paperback
Webster

into the yellow kitchen light
to show me *coriander*.
The bouquet

of cilantro pushed
across the kitchen table,
forks clattered to the floor

and the smell of bread
in the hollow of your neck,
our bodies' weight pressed against

the solid oak, cookbooks
leaving hard angles
in the soft arch of my back.

Stacey Balkun

The plasticglass sound
as the cinnamon jar hits the tile,
the small puff of itself that joins the air

and the dictionary, somehow mixed up
with everything else
on the kitchen table,

now cleaved somewhere between
microcosm and
Millay.

Our two skins, slicked
like tomatoes
in rain.

Our two bellies
now full.

First published in Los Angeles Review, 2013

Dimanche Gras 2009
by Missy Wilkinson

Sunday morning around eight a.m., perhaps one of the most penitent times that exist, Rose calls and wakes me up. I like Rose. She's in her late twenties, like me, and she wears false eyelashes even when she's not at work. She walks around with a perpetually surprised look, thanks in part to her eyebrows, which she tweezes bass-clef thin. I suspect she's mostly an escort who dances on the side, rather than a dancer first and foremost. Not that it makes any difference, as long as I don't have to be part of it.

"Did I wake you up?" The nasal tang of her West Bank accent oozes through the line. Rum for room. Aa-yuss for ass. "Listen, I've got a job for us. Two hundred dollars and all you have to do is rub your boobs in some guy's face for a second before he catches a plane."

"I'll be there in less than an hour."

As I frantically soap up and shave everything from my legs to my perineum, I contemplate my good luck. Less than an hour from now, I'll be back in bed, crisp cash in my hand. There's something talismanic about stripper money that regular direct deposit paychecks can't touch. The way it rides against the flesh of my inner thigh, held there by a metallic silver garter, for hours and hours through the murky, slot-machine illuminated haze of the clubs. Shoes, bikini sets, thongs--everything eventually comes off except for that wad of cash money. I must feel its touch at all times. If I don't, it's because something has gone horribly wrong. When I deposit those bills at the bank, groom them into tidy stacks so as not to inconvenience the teller, I feel as though I've lost something vital.

Hugged by a wraparound porch, the blue mansion on Magazine Street looks stately from the outside, but when I go in, I discover that it's been cut up into little condos. Rose and I find three overgrown frat boys watching *Point Break* and drinking Bud Light. They pay us. We count the money while we change.

I'm beginning to think this is a little more than just boob-smushing.

"Girl, I don't feel like dancing today," Rose says as she straps on her clear plastic stiletto heels. "I wish we could just do something easy, like give the bachelor a hand job."

This is definitely more than boob-smushing.

We do a standard show--get naked, do lap dances. Not a lot of girl-girl stuff and definitely no dildo action--we're only getting $200 each. But the Bachelor feels comfortable enough to take off all his clothes. He's not a bad-looking guy; he kind of reminds me of Matthew Broderick, if Matthew Broderick wore Mardi Gras beads and was really coked out. I wish he'd put his clothes back on, and if it were up to me, he would. But Rose owns this mobile stripper party business, and she's the one who calls the shots. So I keep my mouth shut and my hands far away from his flaccid, coke-whipped penis.

"Hey, come over here," says one of the Bachelor's friends. He turns out to be much less wasted than the Bachelor, and much more clothed. I take him up on the offer. Best men love to wax poetic about the virtues of their bros, so I listen, wide-eyed and encouraging, asking leading questions, while he tells me what a great dude the Bachelor is, how the ladies can't get enough of him. I hope this will net me a tip, but in the end, it doesn't.

Rose summons me to a bedroom and we excuse ourselves to give the Bachelor a "private dance." The private dance consists of me lying on the bed sipping ice water from a plastic Krewe of Bacchus cup while Rose tries to give the Bachelor a hand job.

"Damn, what's wrong with you, baby?" she asks when her efforts fail to bear fruit--or wood. Hah. I never said I wasn't cheesy.

"Mrmghghgh," the Bachelor explains. He keeps clenching his fists and flexing his feet and pulling at Rose's hair even though she told him not to, because it's a wig.

"Huh?" Rose asks.

"He said something about fifteen lines earlier," I supply helpfully.

She squirts sunscreen on his penis, thinking lack of lube was the issue. With a little SPF 30, he should be all ready to go, no doubt. I just want her to be done. This is so not boob smushing. I hate lying here while she does this. This isn't what I thought I was getting into. But I don't leave. Some grim sense of Puritanical work ethic or ingrained fear of authority or innate sluttiness or *something* keeps me lying there.

One thing I could never have predicted about all this: I could never have predicted how many boundaries I actually had, and how going to work would continually test them, stress them and more often than not, break them. The first time a guy came during a lap dance, I totally did not know what was happening until he told me. He seemed pleased about it. I thought, "Well, that was gross, but I'm fine."

Girls always say you need to know your boundaries before getting into this line of work. I knew I wouldn't be okay with jerking someone off, but was I okay with *watching* someone else jerk him off? That's a boundary I never knew I had. I keep discovering (and straining to enforce) new ones; the weight of male desire is as heavy as a grand piano stored in a dusty, termite-ridden attic. Eventually, the floorboards give. The piano keeps falling and falling, and there's no foundation to end its plummet, only an infinite proliferation of split-levels and spiral staircases and crawl spaces and trap doors, because commodified desire is a structure, and men built this, too.

Old-timers say stripping used to be stripping and prostitution used to be prostitution. But now they blend

Condoms and Hot Tubs Don't Mix

together, and maybe Rose the hybrid stripper/prostitute is actually not much of a hybrid at all.

She's given up on coaxing an erection out of him.

"That's a trick I use," she revealed as we changed back into street clothes. "When I know they won't be able to get it up, I offer hand jobs so we don't have to do the girl-girl show."

So now I'm supposed to feel grateful.

Outside, the air is brisk and sun-filled. I almost get mown down by a couple of joggers. All I want is a smoothie, but after fighting parade crowds on Saint Charles Avenue, I see the Smoothie King isn't even open.

Things are getting confusing and annoying--so many crowds! So many police cars! I hate Mardi Gras parades!--and I'm starting to feel very ill, either from hunger or what just happened, I'm not sure which.

There used to be a Smoothie King by the University of New Orleans, but I'm not sure if it's open post-Katrina. I take a gamble and thank God! It's still there.

My car door bumps a truck as I exit and a sweet, zaftig girl asks worriedly if I "hit it hard."

"I barely touched it." I hate people who are so jumpy about their cars. Objects that hurtle around at great speed and in proximity to other objects that also are hurtling around aren't meant to go through life without scratches and dents. They just aren't. So I sort of snarl.

Of course, her stupid boyfriend works at the Smoothie King and she cries to him about how I was rude and as I'm leaving, he asks me to apologize. He just has no fucking idea. I've had nothing to eat, I've had to witness a coked-out hand job, and I'm up way earlier than I need to be. I am mean as a snake but I am trying, trying, to keep it under control. I wasn't even that rude!

"I feel like shit," I say, trying to put it in terms he can understand. "I'm coming down with something."

"Yeah, a lot of people have felt like shit this past weekend," he says, implying that I feel like shit because I've been out drinking and partying like the rest of the city and am therefore culpable.

I think about the worried, round-faced girl. I bet this asshole tells her to lose weight. I bet he makes her drink "Slim Down" smoothies. I bet that she was scared he was going to chew her out or worse for getting his precious truck dinged on her watch. He seems like that kind of guy, the kind who is in love with his truck. I would go so far as to say that he wishes I *had* dinged his truck so he could give me a good tongue-lashing and not just this demand for an apology.

Suddenly, I do feel sorry. Not for the reasons he thinks I should.

"I'm sorry I was so rude to your girlfriend," I say. "Goodbye."

I take my smoothie home and collapse into bed for the next three days with a raging fever and a headache that feels like my cranium is being impaled by an uprooted stop sign. It hurts even when I fall asleep. Costumed skeletons, the Skull and Bones gang, knock on doors and beat the street signs outside my camelback double early Tuesday morning, and I consider getting up to watch the parades. But I fall back asleep. When I awake, Mardi Gras is over, the streets are empty, and the frat boys, whores, bachelors, revelers and jealous lovers have all gone home.

Sexcapade
Sex Fact 1

Vibrators were created to help women relieve a sexual frustration condition known as "hysteria."

Prior to its creation, many women went to doctors or midwives to receive manual treatment, but this labor proved to be exhausting and lead to hand cramps and muscular fatigue.

Clippity-Clop What-Not
by Steve Meador

I was awakened by something subtle like the scuffing of a closing drawer, but it was indistinguishable, as noises generally are during sleep, and it was coupled by an awareness of something near; something akin to a minute electrical charge or a wisp of air that lifted the fine hair on my arms and neck. I did not stir from my position on my right side when I opened my eyes, then closed them instantly after the viewing. Suzie was standing about five or six feet away, near the foot of the bed, naked, her head tilted fully back, her spread fingers running through both sides of her towel-dry hair. Eyes are smart, even when the brain is dull, and will open in the narrowest of slits to peer through hazy lines of eyelashes in order to consume what they want, or what they are conditioned to want. Her small breasts were nearly all nipple, not much more than the conical buds I had felt on Sheila in the seventh grade. Suzie lifted her right hand to toss her hair from her forehead and eyes, and on the return trip her fingers trailed slowly over the deep rose-colored round on her right breast before sliding to her side and moving lower. The turn of her curve from ribs to hips was a completely unexpected pleasure, deeply cut and sloping—the clichéd hourglass. Her near-exclusive wardrobe consisted of bib overalls of different tones, and those had hidden this treasure of coves, caves, and curves. My viewing dribbled lower and there it was—the snapper, the grabber, the mother of all milking devices. Suddenly, it was inching closer, growing darker as it moved toward me, away from the low wattage light on the dresser behind her. In the stupor of half-sleep, I thought of it as a furry Venus flytrap, something sugary that would lure me near, then engulf my face and try to suffocate me—or, perhaps, a giant sooty clam, opening and closing with the power of Doberman jaws. She bent over, pulled open the drawer on the nightstand, and rustled around the inside. Her perfume, Tabu, sent magic tendrils burrowing into my nostrils, delivering a wake-up call to parts of my body that began to crank and stir. Suddenly, the bedroom door opened and Ron, my roommate, came in. I did not move and could hear him hiss at her, "What the *fuck* are you doing?" She whispered, "Looking for a rubber. I don't see one in the drawer." He was a hundred and eighty pounds of bulky pissed off. "For who? Him? Why are you fucking naked?" She remained calm. "He's asleep. What are you mad about, Ronny?" He hated to be called that. "Get some damn clothes on and get out of here." The bickering continued beyond the door after she left the bedroom. I could hear words like slut, whore, and cunt being tossed out, each followed by her soft return of "Sorry." It was Ron who was solely responsible for the blurred staring, with the tales of incredible sex he had with Suzie. There were four of us in the campus apartment and he was constantly feeding Joe, Jeff, and me the spicy pablum about her "snapping pussy." He said it was like sticking a teat cup from an automatic milking machine onto your dick. "You'll moo for an hour!" He would open his hands, place them palm on palm, then shove them toward our faces as he snapped them rapidly, like an alligator's jaw. "Here it comes, boys, LOOK OUT! The labiata clamata is gonna snap ya. Here she comes, here she comes!" That is why I had to peek. I had to see what Ron called "her twit, her twat, her clippity-clop what-not." Maybe he made the whole thing up, or maybe it was everything he had been telling us for months. Maybe she wanted to show me how it worked. Maybe that is why I remained there, motionless, half thrilled, half scared shitless that the thing might fall upon me and suck my eyes out, or roll me on my back, sit on me, and milk me like I was some dairy cow.

Sexcapade Sex Fact 2

Only about 25% of women are consistently orgasmic during penis-in-vagina intercourse. Many women also need clitoral stimulation to achieve orgasm.

Anything But Boredom
by Cecilia M. Fernandez

Withering weeds poked out from the parched soil all over the front yard. Ellen and I side-stepped broken clay pots and dodged brittle branches from craggy trees as we made our way to the wide double doors of a ramshackle house set back at least 100 yards from the street. Ellen, new in school, told me she ran away from her parents in Illinois and had just moved in to this commune on Miller Road in Coral Gables, about a mile from the University of Miami. She wore her blonde hair down to her waist, a beaded suede vest and long stained skirt, definitely a hippie. I was curious about her lifestyle and didn't refuse when she invited me home. It was 1971, and we were both 17.

After the death of my grandparents, more alone than ever, I felt wild, crazy, ready to do anything, craving sensation; they were one of the last ties to the rule and regulation ridden Cuban culture that fell on me like a heap of stones, anchored me in place. None of my friends rejected it like I did, and I didn't know anyone else who was curious about the hippie lifestyle. I pictured American culture as fluid, open; nevertheless, I felt like an outsider in both places. Not only was I a marginalized Cuban immigrant, but I also lived on the outskirts of traditional Little Havana. I wanted wholeness. Was it impossible to unify these two selves?

Inside Ellen's house, a spacious living room welcomed us with mattresses shoved up against the walls, huge pillows and blankets covering the floor. Black lights glowed from every lamp, and psychedelic posters blazed from the walls. Flowered curtains served as doors to rows of small bedrooms. Heavy incense hung in the air, forming masses of clouds in the dim light, colliding with the sharp odor of marijuana. Jimi Hendrix and Janis Joplin howled nonstop from an eight track cassette player on the floor.

Ellen disappeared down a hall, and a man walked up to me. He wore hip hugging bellbottom jeans held up with a wide leather belt and a buckle in the shape of a peace sign. His scrubby T-shirt hung limply on his thin frame.

"You want a drag?" He handed me a joint. I was here because I wanted to shed the heavy cloak of Cuban-ness, step past the barriers and experience…what? Anything but boredom.

The smoke seared my lungs just like the first time with Ovy, but now I felt a slight dizziness and floating sensation; I coughed several times.

The man, much older than me, motioned to one of the small rooms. My heart was beating, and I felt short of breath. We sat on a dirty, sheet-less, sagging mattress in silence. He handed me a water pipe. I put it to my lips and blew smoke out, not inhaling, struggling to clear my head from the effect of the joint.

Soon, we were making out and rolling around, one on top of the other.

Ellen threw herself on the mattress, too. My first experience with spontaneous sex seemed more like a wrestling match than intercourse. For a while, no one knew whose arms or legs were flailing into the air. My heart and soul retreated, but my body continued to function as the nameless man penetrated me, and I reached out to Ellen who was on her knees right next to my head. As my hips gyrated, my mouth locked with hers. Everything felt unnatural.

Another woman announced her presence by rapping on the walls with a wooden ladle. We jumped apart as she began to pour out lemonade into paper cups from a plastic pitcher and line them up on the floor. She waved her hands in the air, threw her head back and howled, already tripping on LSD. Worried the hallucinogic drug would be in the lemonade, I did not drink it. We rapidly pulled on our clothes, and I watched her run out to the common room and gallop around, boomeranging against the walls and yelling.

"Wow, she's on a bad trip," Ellen exclaimed. "But we gotta go," she told the man. "We got school tomorrow." The man walked off, taking the pipe.

I observed Ellen out of the corner of my eye as I followed her to the station wagon, dented on all sides and with one door caved in. She acted as if nothing unusual had happened. I wanted to be just as cool, so I said nothing.

She handed me a Hershey's chocolate bar, and I ate it ravenously. She dug into a bag of chips. I wasn't high anymore, and as we drove, I went over in my mind what I had just experienced. Running off to the commune with Ellen offered a possible escape from Little Havana, but, I realized, not the right path for me. I enjoyed the music, the fashion, the politics; I didn't want to be a hippie. An interesting story to tell my friends, I thought. If I dared.

"See you tomorrow," I said as she dropped me off and screeched away.

Ovy was in the living room and ran out when he heard the car door slam. I didn't expect him to be there, and I felt a bit nervous.

"Where were you?" he shouted, in a jealous frenzy.

"I was just visiting…"

"You smell of smoke!" he screamed, recognizing the pot smell. "Tell me where you were! Tell me the address. I'm going to find out what you were doing and kill them!" He grabbed me by the shoulders, eyes protruding. I shook him off.

I walked to the kitchen and picked up the telephone book. My heart contracted.

"Here," I threw the heavy volume in his direction. "Find it yourself."

Ovy jumped in his car and drove off. The next morning, he called, and we made up. But Ellen was not at school that day. She had no phone, so I couldn't find out her whereabouts, and I did not want to go back to the house.

I never saw her again.

First published as part of the memoir Leaving Little Havana *(Beating Windward Press, 2011)*

Sexcapade Sex Fact 3

Relationship satisfaction is linked to the length of sexual foreplay in both men and women. In particular, older men who rarely, seldom, or never engage in foreplay are more likely to report that sex was not pleasurable and that they had problems with arousal, erection, orgasm, and ejaculation.

Love in the Dark *BABS! the great*

Sexcapade Sex Fact 4

During pregnancy, many women report having "the most intense orgasms of their lives" thanks to increased genital blood flow. Even women who had never experienced orgasms enjoyed them while they were pregnant. However, in some women the increased sexual stimulation was overwhelming sensitive, causing discomfort.

Demon Penis Octopus
by Bethany DuVall

"Have you ever been filled with the Holy Spirit?" Miss Amy would ask.

Tabernacle Church was two storefronts in a strip mall. We were a twice-a-week church family. I'd wake up from pinched-off dreams on Sunday mornings, and spend my last hours before falling into uneasy sleep on Wednesday nights, in these retail-made-holy spaces with metal folding chairs. My parents and Nina and I would stand and clap our hands and raise them in the air and sing Hosanna while Mr. Bob played the electric keyboard at the front. When the music ended and Pastor Ryan got up to talk, I got sent down the covered sidewalk, through the double glass doors where we had children's church and Junior Bible Quiz cards with memory verses on the backs. It wasn't like the quiet churches in Connecticut. I missed the snow.

"Have you ever been filled with the Holy Spirit?" Miss Amy asked, and started praying in baby talk with her arms swaying above her. Miss Amy was Mr. Bob's wife, and since they didn't have any kids, she liked to teach all of us. She called us her surrogates. Once I drew her a picture of curly iron gates that were wide open and all of us kids were inside, even Greg, who nobody liked because he would pinch and pull hair when you weren't looking. I titled it "Sure Gates," and Miss Amy pinned it up on the children's church wall.

When she prayed in baby talk, the edges of her blurred and fuzzed like the trees in a nightmare that had slipped out of place and left a dark emptiness where there were supposed to be branches. A nothing surrounded Miss Amy, too, but this one was bright and left shining colors in my eyes when I closed them, the way the sun did. The colors of Miss Amy glowed sickly green. But when I opened my eyes, she blazed white again, and the other kids were all making baby sounds and rolling back their eyeballs in their heads and some were jumping up and down and some were flat on the floor. They all had the blurry white edges. The ceiling felt too low, a gray cloud hungry to swallow us all in its thunder. The ceiling pressed down on us, and only our hands, filled with the blazing white sick green of the Holy Spirit, could keep it from collapsing. I thrust my palms to the darkening sky and started whispering and humming baby noises, too.

•••

Nina was the pretty one. She'd even had a boyfriend back in Connecticut, but after we moved he graduated high school and married some other girl. Nina wore bubblegum lip gloss and hoop earrings and listened to Pat Benatar. On good days, she would do me up in purple eye shadow. Sometimes even mascara. I threw my eyelids open, afraid to blink, afraid not to blink. My eyes dried out till they burned under the black mascara wand, and Nina's perfect face would go blurry while I dug my fingernails into the soft pads of my hands so she wouldn't see them shaking. "Hold still!" she'd demand, no matter how I tried to control the trembling. With Nina, you never knew if she was going to give you long, lush lashes or try to jab your eye out.

"Don't tell Mom."

Tears streamed down. I wasn't even crying, they were just coming and coming because my eye hurt to open and hurt to close, and it felt like maybe it had come loose a little. Do eyes come loose? Between sloshes of cold water trying to drown the throbbing sting, I caught a glimpse of myself in the bathroom mirror. The white had gone bright red between my iris and my tear duct. The beautiful mascara had smudged into bruises so I looked like a skull with red hair and red eyes. Nina told me it served me right, hunting through her makeup without asking. I deserved to have my eye poked out, and I was lucky she didn't send it rolling across the floor, and maybe she'd think about asking Mom not to ground me if I did exactly as she said for the rest of the afternoon.

•••

At dinner, I stared at my plate and ate quickly. No one asked why I looked like I'd been punched in the eye.

Later that night, Nina breezed through the kitchen in a lavender mini skirt with black polka dots. I kept rinsing dishes and putting them in the dishwasher. She yanked open the refrigerator and pulled out a dark bottle half full of wine. The cork made a hollow sound. I placed another dripping bowl on the rack. Nina stared right in my eyes as she lifted the bottle and took two gulps. Our dog Crackers padded into the kitchen on her tiny white feet. Nina winked at me, squatted down in her heels, and offered Crackers a sniff. Crackers leaned toward the bottle without stepping closer to Nina. Her little neck stretched until her wriggling nose caught the scent. She gave a loud yip and ran off.

Nina stood back up. She stared at me, and I didn't move. She was holding the bottle out to me just like she had with Crackers. I could hear the laugh track on the TV two rooms away, where my parents would be watching together. I took the cold neck of the wine bottle in my solemn hand, and drank.

•••

When Nina got pregnant, Mom told her to move out, but Dad said he'd empty his study to make a nursery. Nina played loud music and refused to go to school. All day, I couldn't hear Mrs. Eshelman's math and handwriting lessons because I was worried about what Nina might do to Crackers while the rest of the family was away. When the mustard colored bus opened its mouth and spit me out at home, I'd burst through the door and pat my knees, calling out Crackers' name till she came running on her rabbit-short legs. Crackers licked all the skin on my face and I felt her over for bruises.

No injuries, but there was clear sticky stuff in the fur near her tail and all over her hind legs. She gave a little yip when I touched it. Hair spray? I sniffed. It had no smell, but bits of blood crusted the furs closest to the base of her tail.

"Sarah! That you, you little shit?"

I scooped up Crackers and tiptoed down the hall. I had to pass Nina's room to get to mine. As we approached her door, Crackers began to shake. I held her closer and told her *shh*. The music behind Nina's door stopped. Crackers whimpered. I gave up tiptoeing and bolted to my room, my backpack jumping up and down on my butt as I went. Nina's door swung open.

"Hey, let me in." Nina leaned against my door, keeping me from closing it those last couple inches. I pushed back from the inside, bracing my feet against my solid oak dresser for leverage. Crackers took cover under my bed.

"I just - want to - ask about your school - day." Weird pauses punctuated Nina's clenched words as she pushed. Her hand snaked through and clawed at my shoulder. She'd be all the way inside in a second if I didn't do something. Crackers let out another whimper.

I couldn't think of anything else. I let myself fall forward, off the door. It was a risk. If Nina was fast enough, she'd shove right in. But I needed space to build momentum. Like a pitcher's wind-up. All my muscles tensed into my legs and back, and I slammed myself as hard as I could against the door.

Nina let out a roar. Her hand disappeared through the small opening, and while she was swearing at me that I'd broken her arm, I locked the door.

"I'm telling Mom what you did to Crackers!" Nina shouted.

•••

Nina got to Dad first. He didn't tell me what he thought I did to our dog, only that I was grounded from playing with her for the rest of the month. And I got a spanking with the wooden spoon. Five swats so hard that my butt was numb by the third one, so I could barely feel the last two. Dad took Crackers to the emergency vet while Nina was assigned to babysit me till Mom got home. I locked my door and curled up in my bed and imagined Nina going on a hot air balloon ride with her huge belly, and falling out, and they could only save the baby. I got to be the big sister. Big Sister Aunt. And I would never poke my little sister in the eye with a mascara wand.

When Mom got home, I could hear Nina right outside my door. "Sarah's grounded. Dad said." Nina wouldn't tell her why.

Later that night, Mom came in my room with a piece of graph paper and a box of maxi pads. She sat down on the corner of my bed and started drawing diagrams.

"This is your uterus," she said, sketching an upside-down triangle with a tentacle coming off each of the top corners. A two-armed octopus. "These are your fallopian tubes and these," she drew little circles at the ends of them, "are your ovaries."

Mom explained menstruation, and she told me that when a man put his penis in a woman's vagina, the eggs could get fertilized and she'd have a baby.

I stared at her. I didn't understand why she was telling me this. "Why are you telling me this?"

Mom's best friend Elsie had gotten her period when they were eight, she explained.

I couldn't remember Mom ever mentioning Elsie before, but I didn't say so. I didn't like it when she talked about her world before me. My world started with me, and it was OK if George Washington and Martin Luther King wanted to do things before I was born, but my mom was my mom. How could anyone have known her before I did? It was bad enough that Nina knew her first, being older. But for Mom to exist before Nina was born, for people to know things about her that I didn't know, set cracks in the ceiling of my world.

Mom went on like it was no big deal, knowing this Elsie before she knew me. No one had had this talk with Elsie. Elsie couldn't figure out how she'd soiled her "Tuesday" panties. It happened again on "Wednesday," "Thursday," and "Friday" before Elsie's mom did the wash and realized that she had some explaining to do for her daughter, who had been too mystified and embarrassed to ask.

Mom didn't want me to be taken off-guard by womanhood.

"So a man put his penis in Nina's vagina?"

Mom's lips pressed into a thin line. "Sarah, did you touch Crackers?"

"I petted her when I came home, but she was all sticky."

Mom closed her eyes and pressed her lips even tighter and nodded. But she kissed my forehead on her way out, so I knew whoever she was angry at, it wasn't me.

I was still grounded, but Mom brought me dinner in my room, and even dessert, which was my favorite: cheesecake. Which we never had, and really never had when we were grounded.

I smooshed the spongy, creamy cake between my tongue and the roof of my mouth and looked in the mirror at my belly, where my octopus-triangle swam beneath my skin, and wondered about my mother's baby recipe: open vagina, insert penis, mix, let sit nine months. It sounded kind of like making a milk shake. Could it really be that simple?

•••

After Nina got pregnant, we stopped going to church. Mom didn't like the way people whispered. Dad would light up and talk about how he was going to be a grandpa. He'd pat Nina on the shoulder and look so proud. Dad saw only Nina, but Mom saw the raised eyebrows and the way conversations shifted when we came into the retail sanctuary. She started staying home on Wednesday nights. She said she was too tired from work. Nina got to ride up front with Dad, and they had a game where they would go through the alphabet and say an insult that started with each letter. Whoever said the best nastiest insult won. *Ancient asswipe. Bug-loving Butthead. Crackhead cocksucker. Dumbass dogfucker.*

"Not funny, Nina," Dad said, glancing at me in the rearview mirror. His eyes made my stomach go knotty.

So that was it? Nina told him I fucked the dog? I wasn't completely clear what fuck meant. It was one of those words I wasn't allowed to use, and that no one used in front of Mom. But the graph paper diagram of my two-armed octopus flashed in my memory. *Sarah, did you touch the dog?* Mom had asked, but now in the backseat of the old Thunderbird, I could almost hear her saying, *Sarah, did you fuck the dog?*

Nina looked down, but I could see the side of her cheek bunching up at the corner of her smile. "Sorry, Dad. I meant dung-eating drag-ass."

I stared out the window. I didn't want to hear any more. Subdivisions with names like Sandy Palms and Wavecrest Place blurred past and mixed with the soundtrack of insults. The car wasn't going too fast, but my eyes were full of tears. *Bulging Bellied Bitch*, I thought. But they were way past the B's, and I wasn't allowed to play anyway.

In children's church, Miss Amy had all the kids lay hands on me to pray out the demon that had got inside my sister. I told her it was a penis, not a demon. Miss Amy looked so shocked I thought her eyeballs might come loose, without even using a mascara wand. I imagined them rolling down her cheeks like marbles and all the kids chasing them around the industrial linoleum floor.

"Boys and girls," she said at last, "our Sarah needs your prayers just as desperately as her wayward sister." She placed one hand on my forehead and one on the back of my neck. "Gather around." And eighteen pairs of hands crawled over me. Miss Amy started talking right to the demon himself that had somehow got inside of me. *No demon shall live in this child. No demon is welcome here. Get out, we command you, in the name of Jesus and Miss Amy and eighteen holy children and one poor soul with a defiled sister. Get out.* And the baby talk commenced. We were a glowing mountain of white and green Holy Spirit faith with nonsense babbling out of us under a ceiling as thick and gray as volcanic ash.

"Get your hands off my daughter." Dad's voice echoed through the storefront church. The voices of my Bible Quiz Cards compatriots went silent. Some of the smaller fingers slipped away from my knees, thighs, ribs. But Miss Amy's grip tightened. At the peak of our praying mountain, she raised her head, eyes closed, toward the smoky ceiling and babbled on, louder and more commanding with each meaningless syllable. I wanted to turn my head to see Dad's face, but Miss Amy held it stationary. Some of the braver kids babbled a little under their breath.

"I said stop." Dad yanked me out from under the mountain. My metal chair clattered to the floor, scattering the children and banging into Miss Amy's shin. I'd never seen Dad so angry. Outside the glass door, Nina stood in her heels and big belly. Her face looked smudgy.

Condoms and Hot Tubs Don't Mix

"That child needs the cleansing of the Holy Spirit!" Miss Amy's voice was shrill. She rubbed her leg. "Her sister's vile act had brought an impure spirit into your house."

Miss Amy threw her words like spit in Dad's face. Dad didn't wipe them off. He didn't move at all. He just glared at her. Miss Amy tried to glare back, but her eyes were going red and then they filled up and then tears started spilling out. Her shoulders collapsed around her neck like a wrecked statue.

Dad's face didn't get any softer. Why was he being so mean to her? It wasn't her fault she didn't know babies came from penises and not demons. Maybe no one ever drew her an octopus diagram.

Dad started walking away. I snatched up my orange pocket New Testament that I had won for being the best at memorizing the Junior Bible Quiz Bonus Bible Verses, and followed.

We were to the door when Miss Amy spoke. "Do you know I can't have children?"

Dad stopped.

Miss Amy was still standing at the top of the church children mountain. "We tried for three years."

My heart beat fast. I could help with this. I could tell her about the penis in the vagina trick. Mom had us two kids, and even Nina had figured it out, and between you and me, Nina acts all bossy and smart, but she's really pretty dumb sometimes. If she could do it, Miss Amy could. I opened my mouth, but the words stuck in my belly. They didn't even make it to my throat. The white light had fled away from Miss Amy, and somewhere in the shadows there seemed to be thoughts and feelings roiling around that I couldn't understand. I could just glimpse them in the corner of my eye, after they'd already shrunk away from me. I was suddenly sure Miss Amy knew the penis trick, but for some reason it hadn't worked for her and Mr. Bob.

"We won't be back," Dad said. But his voice was soft and gentle, like when he sometimes tucked me in at night, and when he read me the voice of the velveteen rabbit when it whispers, *What is Real?*

"Thank you," Miss Amy said, and moved her mouth into something that was almost a smile under her weeping eyes. Dad nodded.

"Let's go, Sarah."

•••

The next Sunday, I wore my lime green skinny strap dress with the ballerina poof skirt. The smell of bacon crept into my room while I was stomping around in Nina's hand-me-down purple bunny slippers pretending to be two giant purple people eaters fighting over who got to eat Strawberry Shortcake and her friend Blueberry Muffin. The salty rich smell interrupted me mid-stomp, saving Blueberry from certain death. I ran out and almost tripped around the corner at the end of the hall. Breakfast was my favorite. We never had hot breakfast on Sundays. It was too much work before church, so we ate cold cereal and toaster waffles. Now that we weren't going to church, were we going to start having cooked breakfasts?

Nina was in the kitchen standing over the skillet. Her belly swelled under a powder blue, ankle-length dress with little flowers on it. I'd never seen the dress before. It looked like a meadow in the sky. I'd never seen her cook before. I decided to proceed with caution.

"Are you making any extra?"

Nina smiled at me. Her eyes were gentle. I felt a little sick. Too many things in one morning that I'd never seen before.

"Your dress is too short," she said. But her voice was quiet. "Go put on something decent. Breakfast is almost ready."

"But Dad said-"

"I'm sorry, I didn't hear you. Did you say you wanted bacon?" Nina plucked up one of the strips already resting on a plate of paper towels, held it above her mouth, and chomped it down. "Better hurry, or there won't be any left."

I yanked off the bunnies so I could run faster and was back in three minutes wearing a sailor dress that came past my knees. For Nina, I put on purple socks because that's her favorite color, and a purple scrunchie. I ate five pieces of bacon and one buttered toast while she brushed my hair and rearranged the scrunchie.

•••

"Are we going to get in trouble?" I asked.

Nina turned up the praise hymns on the radio. A banjo plucked away while twangy voices sang about an unbroken circle.

She had let me sit in the passenger seat of Dad's Thunderbird, but I was getting a little car sick, or bacon sick, and nervous about going to church when Dad had told Miss Amy we wouldn't. Were we really carrying demons? And why did it matter that Miss Amy and Mr. Bob couldn't have kids?

"Did Dad say you could borrow the car?"

"Did you like the bacon?" Nina asked. I felt a lot more car sick.

"You don't even like church," I said.

"Don't ever say that. I have to go to church. How else am I going to make up for this?" Nina gestured at her belly.

"You mean the demon?"

Nina would have laughed at demons six months ago. Now she looked grim.

"Nina, it's not a demon. It's a penis. Mom says when you let a penis get in your vagina-"

Nina's palm slammed into my cheekbone. My head thunked against the car door, and a thousand fireflies lit up my eyes, then vanished into tears that I tried to keep from falling.

"Don't talk like that," Nina said.

There's a better home a-waiting in the sky, Lord, in the sky, the radio sang out. I rubbed my head and stared up at the clear blue sky. It felt empty.

Condoms and Hot Tubs Don't Mix

Nina sighed. "Sorry Muppet."

Muppet is what she used to call me when she was in a mood to really like me. She said it all the time when we lived in Connecticut, but she hadn't called me that since we moved to Florida. My stomach knots unraveled a little, and I dared to look at her.

"You're right," she said. "It was a penis. But it's a demon that made me let it in. You're not supposed to let a penis in unless you're married to the guy it is attached to."

"Oh."

"Now no one will want me."

"I want you."

"No man will want me."

"Oh." This was a lot more complicated than Mom's diagram. "What about the penis guy. The one attached to it? Can't you just get married now?"

"No."

"But no one else will want him either, right? Because he already put it in a… you know. So you're perfect for each other."

"It doesn't work like that for men." Nina looked sad. It made her face seem naked. She could look angry or happy or full of trouble, but I'd never seen her just sad. "Besides," she said, "he's already married."

Suddenly I didn't want to go to church. I didn't want to know any more answers, and I didn't want to see Miss Amy whose vagina didn't work. I didn't want to know who the penis guy was married to. I figured I already knew, but if no one said it, then it was just a guess. People guess wrong all the time.

"Can we go home?"

Nina didn't answer.

"How about the beach? I bet the beach is great right now." Nina loved the beach. Dad always said the beach loved her back. It could be the cloudiest day, or a jellyfish swarm reported on the news, or any other disaster, but when Nina stepped onto the sand, the sky cleared and the jellyfish made way. *The beach loves you back,* Dad would say, and Nina would say good because it was the only thing in stupid Florida that did.

"The beach loves you back," I reminded her. I could see she was thinking about it, so I threw out my best offer. "I'll use my allowance tithes to buy us lunch."

Nina glanced at me. "How much have you got?"

"A dollar fifty."

Nina started laughing.

I could feel my face burning. I glared at the flat road winding past a neighborhood called Coconut Terrace. "It's tithes for the whole month."

Nina stopped at the light for East Las Olas, my favorite road because it sounded exotic. Maybe if the baby was a girl, she could name it Las Olas. Or a boy. Was Las Olas for boys or girls? But more than how it sounded, I loved East Las Olas because it led to the ocean.

"Okay, Muppet, I'll make you a deal," Nina said. "I'll buy lunch if you promise to be good."

A wave of relief washed over me. "I'll use my very best manners."

"I don't mean use your manners." She reached over and put a hand on my belly, the same hand that had smashed my head into the door minutes earlier. "I mean, you promise me that you'll be good. Always."

Nina's eyes were sharp and smart, smarter than I knew she could be, in that look she gave me from the driver's seat of Dad's car. Like she was seeing into my future, determined to wash it clean.

The light turned green. Nina didn't move.

A car pulled up behind us. The driver honked, then gave up, speeding around us with a scowl.

The light turned yellow. It reminded me of the sickly way Miss Amy glowed when she prayed and how badly she wanted children, and, I realized, how badly Nina didn't. Why had she let a penis in if she didn't want a baby?

The light turned red.

I stared down at her hand on my stomach. I wasn't the least bit interested in penises just then, not as anything more than theoretical baby ingredients. But I was old enough to know that *always* was a very long time.

The light for the crossroad went yellow. My sister looked back at the road. I realized she was ready to drive straight on to church and Miss Amy's sad empty belly when our side went green again.

"Nina," I said.

"Hmm?" she didn't turn her head.

I patted her hand, pressing it gently into my abdomen, my promised parts.

Nina smiled like the curved lip of a conch shell, pink and a little crooked and full of the ocean's secrets. She flipped on her blinker and pointed us east.

The Lay at Gay Days
by Jameson Tabard

The month before the gays come to town, it's important to watch the diet. I tried to follow this scripture. It was spoken by God to the apostles Adam and Steve, two buff angels who dutifully canonized gay law. That's what I'd been thinking the month before Gay Days, an annual weekend party hosted at and around Disney World.

The color of the day was red. Gay men flaunted their hard-earned bodies in skimpy red tank tops or tight red t-shirts, all in the name of solidarity, unity—and sex. With the influx of no-strings fresh meat, I had one mission: get laid.

Dick o'clock came earlier during Gay Days than any other weekend. A Saturday afternoon pool party kept the cheap alcohol running like a Roman aqueduct, and every man wanted to be seen shirtless to reel in their trick for the night. I arrived late to one shindig, hoping the hot guys were at least three drinks in. That way, their booze-goggles obscured my mortal sin of indulging in one too many burgers.

There was flirting. Imbibing. Some light conversation. I didn't know if it was a bourbon haze or if something was in the air, but my vision did seem to blur a bit. I noticed a slight itch. I made for the bathroom and looked in the mirror. A slight pinkness encroached my right eye. I prayed it wasn't pinkeye. Nothing stymied getting laid like infectious conjunctivitis. I washed my hands well and flushed out my eye with tap water. In Florida, that could make things worse. I don't know what I was thinking.

I waited in the bathroom for a few minutes, staring at myself, willing the pinkness to blanche. The eye seemed to numb, but the damage to my game was done. I resigned myself to finding action at home, where I could take to the hookup sites.

A whole other party raged in cyberspace. It was the place where introverts cruised and found their flings. I'd scanned a few profiles, searching for someone, hoping someone was searching for me. A picture of a dark-haired stud caught my attention. He had soft hazel eyes and long lashes, chiseled cheekbones and smooth skin. I clicked on the additional pictures. Normally, I wanted to read a little more about a person first before I browse, but this wasn't one of those weekends. Conversation, if it ever happened, would have the depth of a teaspoon. This was hook-up time.

One of the obligatory shirtless pics showed a nice sculpted physique. Decent pecs. A faint trace of abs under a light happy trail. This guy might be the one. I sent a message.

Hey. You having a good night?

Asking a question was key—a conversation starter. Most often, replies were seldom, and if they did give one, it would take a while. Nobody wanted to come off as desperate.

This wasn't just anybody. The response came within thirty seconds.

Yeah—not too bad. You?
Great. You doing the Gay Days stuff?
Yeah. Earlier. Chillin' in the hotel room now.

He got to the point quickly. Mentioning the hotel cut right to the chase. He wasn't put off my lack of shirtless pics—or nudes. Normally, guys wanted to preview the goods. I know I did.

You staying at the host hotel?
Nah. Just up the road. The Gardenside.

Phew. Not that I had anything against the host hotel, but going up and down those elevators to the rooms was a meat market, and nine out of ten guys was either on their way to a fuck or leaving one. A different hotel felt a little less conspicuous.

Before I could responsd, he sent another message.

You should keep me company. Room 405.

This guy was perfect. No strings. No inane questions. He knew what he wanted, and he wanted me. Right now.

I'll be there in 30 mins.

I closed my laptop and hopped in the shower, cleansing myself of the grimy mix of sunblock and sweat that'd clung to my skin since earlier in the day. When I was finished, I wiped the mirror of its excess steam and stared at my right eye. The white around the eyeball looked healthy, but just to be safe, I bathed it in antihistamine drops.

I threw on a loose tank top and some mesh gym shorts. My outfit reeked of confidence—perhaps more confidence than I should've had.

The drive to The Gardenside felt longer than it should have, its duration laughing and teasing my crotch. I said thirty minutes, and traffic was threatening to make me a liar. Liars didn't get laid. They show up after the guy has left to find somebody else. I finally parked and scurried passed a smiling bellboy outside. I jetted into an elevator as it was about to close.

When I got to the fourth floor, I stepped out. My breath was heavy as I saw my reflection in a giant Art Deco mirror. I loomed closer to examine my eye, ensuring it was clear to proceed.

As I hurried down the hall, I attempted to slow my breathing. My heart raced. When I reached the room, I knocked lightly.

A pause. The guy took his time answering, maybe ogling me through the peephole to see if I met his standards. Or maybe this wasn't his room at all. For all I knew, this was a set up of some kind. Catfishing. A fake profile.

The door opened slowly, his head peeking around. His eyes smiled, and he gestured for me to come in. He must have liked what he saw. At the very least, I looked enough like my pics. He did too.

As I stepped inside, he locked the door behind us. The dimly lit room was standard. No frills. Generic furniture. The one light beside the bed revealed a tacky painting of seashells over the spot where I assumed we'd be fucking. I seemed to be standing in the shadows, which was preferable to undress in.

Before he turned off the light, I got a glimpse of him. A lean, toned body under a black t-shirt. Defined legs with a moderate amount of hair shot out of his red plaid boxers.

The neon from a nearby building bled through the curtains, coating him in a reddish hue. He whipped off his shirt and flexed his abs. They were better than his online pics promised. I stepped closer and traced my fingers over them. I wanted to smell him, but the stench of Drakkar Noir stung in my nose. I didn't know anyone who still wore that, let alone bathed in it. I tried not to show my distaste by allowing my hand to slip under the elastic band of his boxers.

I grabbed his member—an average-sized one—at the same time his hand explored mine. Our lips met in a soft kiss, his potent Listerine flavor masking a subtle hint of smoke. He pushed me down onto the bed and slipped off my pants, his too-fresh mouth burning my cock with a frigid burst of wintergreen moisture. He slipped his hand under my shirt as he took me all the way in to the back of his throat, massaging me with his soft palate.

I acclimated to his frosty mouth and moaned, his impeccable skill hurrying me to the finish line. He devoured me, tasting every inch as his hands migrated from my chest. As he stroked and sucked, I felt the blood coursing through my veins, pushing me to the brink.

"I'm getting close."

He didn't let up. He kept at it, bobbing up and down as if I were the last man he'd ever be with.

"I'm-I'm-."

He let go, stroking me to finish. A jet of cum shot out of me and landed in my right eye. I winced, my head turning to the side as my cock continued to shoot.

"You okay?" he asked.

"Yeah. I… Do you have a towel?"

He disappeared into the bathroom and remerged with a stiff, over-bleached washcloth. Though he didn't bother to wet it, I found solace in his politeness.

I stood up and gestured to the bathroom. "Can I just-?"

"Yeah."

I stood before the bathroom sink, wetting the washcloth and dabbing the eye. No antihistamine was going to be strong enough to thwart that redness. It was there to stay for a while. I took a deep breath and stepped back out to see the guy—whose name still eluded me. Somehow, some way, I was determined not to let my poor aim ruin the night. He still needed to get off.

The overhead light was harsh and startling.

He lay in the middle of the bed sans shirt, a pillow cushioning his back against the headboard. He smiled and motioned for me to crawl into bed. I felt the wave of relief cleanse my body of any anxiety. He scooted over and propped up a pillow. This guy wanted to talk to me. Have a conversation. It actually felt romantic.

I climbed into bed and sat beside him, my back relaxing into the pillow. I looked at him and smiled. He smiled back—for a split second. His brow furrowed as he looked me in the eye.

"Are you okay?" He asked.

"I feel fine."

He stared at me for a few seconds. "You know what? It's getting kind of late."

"It's only 9:00."

He paused for a moment. Then: "Yeah, but I'm gonna meet some friends and go out dancing."

I nodded my head and stood up, throwing on my clothes and forcing a polite smile. "Nice to meet you, buddy."

I walked to the door and closed it behind me. As I crept toward the elevators, I told myself I'd never do this again. No more lays at Gay Days.

I pushed the down button and turned to look at myself in the mirror. There, under the glare of the fluorescent lights, I saw the redness in my eye, the image seared in my memory as the night I realized I had no aim—and no game.

Sexcapade Sex Fact 5

The average volume of ejaculate for men is roughly three-quarters of a teaspoonful, which is equivalent to one-fourth of a tablespoon or just under 4 milliliters. That's about the volume of a sliver of butter on bread!

Having
by Timothy DeLizza

Ariana pulled down her lower eyelid and lined the inside of the lid from corner to corner using a soft, black, fat-tipped eyeliner. After the lower lid was done, she waved her hand over her eyelid to wave away the pain.

Then, looking upwards, she did the same to the upper lid – lining the inside of her upper eyelid, just where the pink flesh meets the eyelashes.

"Fuck," she said, then bit her hand and blinked away the sting.

She smiled into her bathroom mirror to see how it looked while smiling. A little of the black drifted over the surface of her eyelids, creating an effect Joshua had described as *smokey* the other time she had done it. She had hoped for *sultry*, but even the imaginary Joshua in her mind did not use words like *sultry*.

"That's what you get for dating a hippie schoolteacher," she said, and laughed to herself.

She heard keys rattle and her apartment door open, and then the sound of Joshua walking into the kitchen.

"Are you ready?" she asked, as she struggled with a faux-pearl earring.

Joshua appeared in the mirror. She continued to look at herself. He touched her stomach, and kissed the air in an apparent attempt to kiss her shoulder.

"What's up?" she asked. His hand was cold.

"Leila and Steve broke up," he said.

"When?" she asked.

"About a month ago."

"And she told you today?"

Joshua shrugged. "I hadn't seen her in a while."

Ariana, who had seen Leila briefly the week before, had not heard this. "Did she say anything else?"

Only after these words were out did Ariana notice Joshua's hand, now warm, was shaking against her stomach.

"It was a fairly mutual break up. They'll try to be friends in a month or so."

Ariana turned to face him, to see if he was about to break up with her. She felt a fear, wholly new to their five months of dating. In a moment, her sense of complete control was shattered.

Joshua tried to kiss her, but she blocked him with her hand so that he kissed her palm.

"I don't want to mess up the makeup," she said. "We have to meet Kim and her boyfriend at the restaurant in fifteen minutes."

Joshua looked at her blankly.

"You can mess it up tonight. All you want. When we get back," she said.

He nodded, but looked like he would cry.

"Is everything alright?" she asked, trying to put on the second earring as casually as possible. "I know you care about Leila a lot, is she taking it okay?"

Joshua took a step back, and leaned against the doorway of the bathroom. Ariana turned back to the mirror.

"It's fine," he said. "She's fine. I just – I missed you a lot while she and I were talking."

She looked down, then up to his eyes in the mirror. His whole body was shaking, and she felt an unexpected panic.

"Joshua, what's wrong?"

"Nothing," he said, "I just really— I need to make love to you right now."

"Can't it wait? The restaurant."

He looked down, and shook his head. She turned, grabbed his chin and lifted his head so he had to look at her.

"Give me a second," she said. She walked past him and picked up her cellphone from the kitchen counter. On the dining table, she saw he had brought her sunflowers. Sunflowers! Her favorite.

He's lucky, she thought, smiling at the flowers and letting her fingers graze the pedals as she dialed.

"Hi, Kim… Yeah, it's me. I'm just calling to let you know Joshua and I are running late. Joshua's run into some – about half an hour. No, we'll be there. Okay, bye."

She paused with the phone in her hand, went to the bedroom and applied lubricant, then returned to Joshua, who had not moved from the doorway. He was breathing heavily, and only then did she realize so was she.

"Kim said. Kim said they hadn't gotten there yet, and they'd just spend some time at the bar," Ariana said.

"Thanks," Joshua said.

"Okay." She rubbed into his shoulder with her thumb, then hiked up her dress. "Do you want to—" He grabbed beneath her dress and pulled down her underwear. "Just don't – no kissing – I just – don't want to mess up the makeup."

He nodded, and she felt herself pushed against the wood of the bathroom door. Within moments, he was inside of her. His hands cupped her neck, where he normally placed them when they kissed. He obeyed her instructions, and only looked at her.

She felt four things at once. First was that even with the lubricant she felt some pain because she wasn't fully warmed up, causing an emotionally confusing effect of being physically hurt by her chosen partner during intimacy. Second, which increased as her body warmed and the pain subsided, was a fear of tearing her dress. The dress was hiked up as far as possible, but she felt it stretch against her each time he thrusted. Third was an insistent internal voice repeating *he didn't cheat on me, he didn't cheat on me.* Fourth was an unpleasant fear that she had fallen in love without intending to or consenting to it or wanting to be so vulnerable.

Sooner than she expected, he collapsed onto her shoulder inelegantly. His body felt made of clay.

"It's okay," she said. "It's okay. It's okay."

"Thank you," he said. He sniffed. She stroked his hair.

"Do you need to stay here?" she asked, letting her dress fall back down, but leaving her underwear around her ankles.

"I'll be okay in a second," he said.

She looked at herself in the bathroom mirror. Her sweat and his slight touches had made her makeup a little messy, but not unmanageable.

Joshua stood upright. "I'm just going to change into my suit quickly."

"You brought a suit?" she asked.

"It's in the kitchen."

He disappeared and reappeared wearing the suit.

•••

They walked to the parking lot beneath her building. The lot was cold and she regretted forgetting to bring a jacket but didn't want to be any later.

"Do you want to put your bike inside the car?" she asked, noticing it locked against the far corner.

"I'll pick it up when we come back."

She felt like they were about to have a fight, but she wanted to get to the restaurant. Joshua took the driver's seat without asking, something he had not done before. She got into the passenger seat without a word.

Her fingers were chilly and shaking as she tried to get the passenger belt buckle to work.

"Shit," she said, letting the buckle drop. The buckle snapped back towards the window. She covered her face with her hands and felt stars float wildly in her head.

She opened the passenger door and shut it again. She tried the seatbelt again, and this time it worked.

"Okay," she said.

As soon as the car moved, her eyes started tearing. She looked out the window, so Joshua could not see.

"Why is this dinner important again?" Joshua asked.

"Kim got a job at Goldman Sachs. The one she wanted for years," she said.

"Ariana, are you, are you crying?"

"Yes," she said. Admitting this made her cry harder. "What the fuck just happened up there?"

"I just missed you and I wanted to make love to you. Badly. Very, very badly."

"Did you ask Leila out?"

"A long time ago. You knew."

"At lunch. I mean did you cheat on me? Did you ask her out?"

"No. No!"

Joshua pulled the car over to the side of the road.

"Look. She called you and asked you to have lunch so she could tell you. Why didn't she tell me first?"

"No, I don't think – she's your friend too. She introduced us. She probably didn't tell you because . . . she didn't want people to know until she was certain it was over."

"She only introduced us because Steve was jealous. I just thought you might of. I mean I know you've got more in common – than us. I mean both teachers together, you share lessons plans over the phone. I'm sorry. I'm sorry. Fuck."

Joshua pulled her towards him. At first she thought he was attempting an awkward hug. Instead she went down into his lap, and he cradled her there and let her sob. He touched her face.

"Stop it," she said to herself. Her sobbing noises stopped, but the tears continued silently.

"Did you really think I would cheat on you, then come to your apartment and . . ." he asked.

She scratched his leg then patted it. She thought of the pain of the cold sex earlier. He was typically overly careful with her body. It seemed unlike him.

"Okay, I'm sorry," she said. "You were just so intense in the apartment, and you didn't explain. I still don't know what you were thinking. I was never afraid of losing you before."

His body physically reacted to her last sentence in a way that told her that she had just revealed more than she intended.

"But you're afraid of losing me now?" he asked.

"I'm afraid of losing you now," she said. She squeezed his leg.

He pulled a clump of her hair together in tight fist. "I guess that's fair," he said. "At lunch I was thinking that I – that here I am eating with a woman I wanted to date for years. I don't know what she would have said if I asked her out, but I wanted you – I chose you. Ariana, I chose you."

She stayed on his lap a moment longer, then remembered he couldn't drive while she was like this, and lifted herself back up.

•••

Kim and her boyfriend already had appetizers at the table when they arrived

"I'm just going to make a quick, a quick business call," Joshua said. "Kim, I'm so sorry we're late."

Kim smiled up at Joshua coldly.

"I'll order for us," Ariana said, sitting.

"Is everything okay?" Kim asked, as soon as Joshua was gone.

"Yeah," Ariana said. She watched Joshua as he walked to the hallway where the bathrooms were, and took out his cellphone next to the restaurant's payphones.

"Did he hit you?" Kim asked.

"What?" Ariana said, as the question slowly registered. "No, no, no, we just, we just talked. I was – it was – just – excuse me, could you just order us some red wine, and the pasta with clams."

"He's not good enough for her," Kim said to her boyfriend, just loud enough for Ariana to hear as she walked away.

Ariana smiled as she walked past Joshua. Joshua smiled back.

She stepped into one of the bathrooms. Her eyes were bloodshot and her makeup was completely ruined. Rivers of skin showed where her tears had been. Two thick lines of black eyeliner ran next to them.

Ariana turned on the faucet and washed the makeup off. Her head felt full of cobwebs that were tingling with a pleasant dull throb.

She exited and outside, by the payphones, Joshua was hanging up his cellphone. She hugged him, and whispered in his ear, "Listen to me. Swear. If you don't fuck me again tonight I swear to God I will hate you forever. I'll never forgive you. I'll leave and die and swear to me, swear to me."

"I swear," he whispered back.

"Swear again. Swear."

"I swear," he said.

Sexcapade Sex Fact 6

A majority of men and women report conducting some sort of pubic hair grooming on themselves. Of these groomers, just over one quarter of them reported sustaining a grooming-related injury, such as sustaining a laceration, burn, or rash. Common areas for these injuries in men were the scrotum, penis, and pubis, whereas for women, the injuries were most commonly the pubis, inner thigh, labia majora, and perineum.

Ouch!

A Natural Desire   *BABS! the great*

Sexcapade Sex Fact 7

Although 20%-30% of men report having issues with premature ejaculation, it may be completely normal (especially for young men) and may not require pharmaceutical intervention.

Condoms and Hot Tubs Don't Mix

Watching Porn with My Mother
by Peter M. Gordon

I plump her pillows so she can sit up straighter.
My computer emits tinny rhythmic groans.
She rides the volume control with one swollen hand.
Extracts cigarettes from a blue pack with the other.

"It don't feel right to watch without a drag."
She exhales smoke straight up, watches
tendrils waft around her IV lines
like ghosts reaching through a wall.

Mom tamps her ash on the bedrails.
"Put this out for me, sweetie."
She rubs her dry groin lightly
Clicks the picture size to maximum

"If your Dad had a schlong like that
we'd still be together
Even though he's dead."
At least I got her to use the internet.

She closes her eyes and snores.
Halo of white hair circles her head.
I empty her ashtray.
Extinguish her light.

First published in Two Car Garage (CHB Media, 2011)

Sexcapade
Sex Fact 8

Despite the rise of the Internet, consumption of pornography actually hasn't increased much over time. Thirty-two percent of men indicated they had watched pornography in the decade before the Internet (1987-1997). That figure rose only two percent for men surveyed in the dozen years after the rise of the Internet (1998-2010).

Paper Cranes
by Alex Celine

It's about six and my suite mate Nicole and I are baking cookies for her class's final exam tonight. She is in the kitchen just down the hall from where I stand now, at Nick's door. This gives me my chance, the one I hadn't even let myself hope for, but the idea was sitting there in the back of my head waiting to appear at the right moment.

"How's it going?" I ask as I lean into the open door of his dorm room. I hadn't planned to do what I am about to, only hoped that I would get a chance to say goodbye before we both left.

"Hey, Ava," Nick says, glancing up from his cleaning. His loud music drowns out his voice.

"What are you doing tonight?" I blurt the words before I can chicken out.

"Huh?" He leaves his dusting rag on the empty desk. He's almost done packing. The only decoration left in Nick's room is the strand of blue lights above the window. I haven't begun to pack yet myself. I don't want to go home. I'm not ready for the year to be over, but the emptiness of the dorm and campus doesn't leave me any fantasy that tomorrow is another day of classes. That there is more time.

Nick walks over and peers out his door and down the hall in both directions. His roommate left right before I came up. He was carrying a box and should be back to the room any minute to continue his packing. My own roommate, Katie, left for good this morning, meaning I have the room to myself tonight.

I watch as Nick walks a few feet around the corner and waves me over to the common area next to his room. I can smell Nicole's cookies baking in the kitchen, but the door is closed and she thinks I'm still changing my laundry over to the dryer.

"We can talk here," he says. I fiddle with my fingers for half a second before I force myself to stop and look at him. The last time we saw each other was a few days ago in the library. Neither of us said a word. He just stood behind me for a few minutes holding my shoulders before I looked up at him. He stepped back and then turned to walk away. This was a few days after I told him I'd decided to go to Scotland next fall, meaning I wouldn't see him for the next eight months. Meaning the thought that we might be more than friends, would never be anything more than that.

"What are you doing tonight?" I ask again. Now that it's said twice and I know he's heard I can't back out.

"I don't have any plans." Across the room there are three tables pushed together with a sign saying 'unwanted items.' They are filled with various things ranging from a box of about fifty Red Bulls to a mini fridge sitting on the floor.

"My roommate's gone," I say and pause for a second. "I was wondering if you'd want to hang out later."

"Like over there? In your room?"

"Yeah."

"Sure," he says. "Where... Where's your room?"

"Second hall."

"You've got my number right?"

I nod. Of course I have his number.

"Okay, well text me later then," he says.

•••

It's ten before I text him. It's a short conversation, my asking if he's still up for hanging out, him asking what my room number is and my telling him, then him saying 'soonish' and adding a smiley face. He comes over twenty minutes later.

"You know how I know you're fun?" he says as he walks in and I close the door behind him. "You have a lime green rug."

Nick rubs his hands together as he looks around, "Wow," he starts counting the paper cranes that are set on three strands of fishing wire strung across the room. "three, four, five..." he moves across the room following the strands and counting all the way to 50 before I stop him and tell him there are 100.

"When you make 100 you get a wish. Katie and I made them."

"Pretty sure it's a 1000 for a wish." He takes his keys and phone out of his pocket and places them on my desk.

"I thought it was 100." I lean back against my bed and pull myself up to sit on it as he begins studying my books. With the number of times I've been in his room, I always wondered what he would think of mine, it's just never came to be before now.

He reads every name to himself, his fingers tracing the titles on the small wooden bookshelf next to my desk. When he finishes, he crosses the room and peers down at the purple plastic box sitting on my dresser. "What's this?"

"Make up."

He picks up the white masquerade mask sitting next to it. It sparkles in the light.

"You're such a girl." He holds the mask to his eyes and finally looks at me. "Is this your disguise?"

I watch his every motion. "No, my little sister gave it to me."

"Hmm, I thought it might be part of your little innocent act. Well you're gonna have to prove that you're not a child."

"And how do I do that?"

"Figure it out. Use your imagination." He puts his hands on my dresser drawer. "What do you have in here? Actually I don't want to open the first drawer. Girls keep strange things in the first one." He opens the second drawer and glances down at my tank tops, closes it, and crosses back to my desk. He picks up my silver jewelry box and opens it. He pulls out a horseshoe necklace.

"My friend made that for me."

He takes a step toward me still holding the small box. It falls to the floor through his fingers and he drops down quickly, apologizing as I slide off the bed to help him. He places the box back on my desk and I wish I could just sit him down for a second, tell him to breathe.

I lean against the bed and he turns to look at me holding the horseshoe necklace out. "Now what were you saying about this one?"

"I don't wear it much." I rest the cold charm against my palm. "But it's special. Her mom owns a jewelry business and she wanted to do something nice for my birthday; she messed up here with the holes." I take the necklace from him and slide myself back onto my bed. I lean over to put the necklace on my dresser before I turn back to Nick who is now looking through my closet.

"These all your clothes?" he asks me. If I walk over to him and hold his arms I wonder if that will keep him still for even a second.

"Only my dresses."

"This one could be for like a circus performer." He pulls out a blue spotted one to look at it before he crosses back to the other side of the room. He picks up the small bottle of bubbles that came in the Finals Week care package from my mom.

"I love bubbles, they're my favorite." He untwists the white top and makes a hole in the silver seal before searching for the wand.

Nick comes back and sits down at the desk chair, the one that used to live under my bed. I took it out after Katie moved to make the room seem less empty. Nick continues to blow bubbles and he catches one on the end then blows again, causing a bigger bubble to appear.

I reach my hand out and pop them as I shift closer to where he is. "What happened to your leg?" I point to a large scab that covers his left knee.

He blows another line of bubbles. "I'm good on my knees," he stands up looking at his hands.

"Nice."

"Your bubbles are getting all over my hands."

Before he can start fidgeting again, I try to come up with some ideas to calm him, but he walks over and wipes his hands on my leg. His fingers are cold against my thigh. The soap smells like plastic.

"There we go." He rubs his hands right at the edge of my shorts and down my thighs a few times before going back to sit on the chair. "Want to hear a sad story?"

"Sure, why not." I lean forward and he blows more bubbles into the space between us.

"Okay. There was a boy and girl. They didn't know each other, but met in a mall. They walked from opposite directions going towards each other and it was like this crazy magnet was pulling them together. They passed by and both of them stopped. They turn to look at each other realizing that they have this hundred percent connection. They weren't at just any mall though, it was a fun mall, with a roller coaster and stuff, so the girl and boy, they spend the day together, eating ice cream and having fun. The end of the day comes and they say that since they have a once in a life time connection, they have to be sure it's meant to be, so they'll just live their lives and the next time they see each other they'll get married the same day."

I press my lips together and nod my head. "Okay," I drag the word out as he meets my eyes. At least he isn't running around touching everything like a three-year-old anymore.

"So they go through their lives, date other people, they find 60, and 70 percent connections, not the hundred they had with each other but still good. And then they marry other people, have children and grandchildren. They end up in the same hospital when they are old and close to death, both on IV's, and they walk down the hall coming from opposite directions. They pass each other, recognizing that it's them, and neither of them looks back."

"It didn't matter anymore. They were almost dead."

"The moral of the story," he tells me. "Is not to split your lottery ticket."

I lean back a little. Nick blows bubbles and looks up to meet my eyes as a shower pours out of the wand. They slowly circulate between us before falling to the floor.

"My hands are all sticky again." Nick stands up and wipes his hands on my bare arms and down my legs yet again before glancing up at the cranes. He reaches up plucking the string so every crane on that strand shutters before he sits back on the chair.

"Ava," he tells me. "The ball's in your court."

We sit for a few minutes as I look around the half empty room, missing all of Katie's decoration that used to tie the room together.

"Here, I'll teach you how to blow really nice ones." He stands in front of me and holds the bubble wand to my lips.

I look into his eyes as I lean forward to blow a line of bubbles into the room past him. He lowers the wand and our faces are about three inches apart. He touches my chin, lifting it slightly. "Perfect form," he says. "You've had a lot of practice."

"Prove it," I tell him and he laughs at me.

"Most girls wouldn't contradict that."

"And most guys wouldn't admit to being on their knees a lot."

"I don't know about that. You ever have someone do it?" He blows more bubbles. I look away from him. "Your roommate left already?" He asks.

"Yeah, this morning."

"How was it when she'd bring guys back?"

"She didn't. She'd usually leave."

"What about your suitemates. Do you know them?" he asks. "Mine are all more roommates really, since we basically all live together."

"I'd think with three roommates instead of one it would be more of a spectacle."

He laughs. "I'm the only spectacle among them. But they learned to deal with it pretty quick. So have you ever had anyone do it?" He blows another line of bubbles. "What are you thinking about?"

"I'm thinking about a few things. First off, I'm trying to decide how honest to be with you, but no, I haven't."

"Interesting. Most girls would now expect the guy to say something along the lines of 'let me show you.'" He blows another line of bubbles, this time up so they float around the cranes before falling back to us.

"Well, I'm also still reeling from that story of yours."

He laughs as he comes back over to me and wipes his hands on my thighs. "It's my goal tonight to make you wet and sticky."

I press my lips together. He sits back on the chair and tries to blow through the bubble wand again, but none make it out this time.

"I'm gonna end up using all of your bubbles." He places them on the desk and stands up. "There enough room on that bed for two?"

I move over and he climbs up next to me. He pulls the blinds out of the way and peaks out into the darkness before dropping them back. Our legs are touching and he reaches over taking my hand.

He closes his fingers around mine for a second and then drops it. "I'm gonna go to the other side."

He puts one hand across me using it to hold his weight as he climbs over. He pauses right above me and our eyes lock. His eyes are so dark. I feel myself holding my breath, but I can't seem to force myself to breathe. It would be so easy to kiss him right now. I could reach up and touch his dark hair, but my hands are frozen by my side. They don't want to move.

The extra seconds he gives me are up and he sits next to me again arms and legs pressed against mine.

"What is it that you want to do," I ask him. "When you graduate?"

"Where do I see myself in five years?"

There is a loud noise from his phone sitting on my desk that sounds through my room, but we hold eye contact.

"Your phone?" he asks.

"No," I shake my head. "My phone doesn't make noise anymore."

"Katie's phone?"

"No, it's yours."

"Oh," he says finally breaking the eye contact and looking away from me. "I forgot I brought it for the alarm. It's later than I thought." I look over at my clock and see that it's eleven thirty. "I have to email an icebreaker homework assignment for my summer class by midnight."

He slowly slides off the bed and walks over to stop his phone as it makes the same obnoxious noise once again. Shutting it off, he puts it in his pocket.

"Goodbye, Ava." He comes over and gives me a hug as I lean off the bed.

I close my eyes as I feel his arms around me. "Goodbye, Nick," I say softly.

•••

I snap the purple jelly case off of one corner of my phone, revealing the blue underneath then secure it back on. "I can bring him back," I tell Nicole, staring at the dark screen.

"What?" Nicole asks me from where she sits under the fuzzy blanket in her bed. The two beds are pushed up next to each other. The one I'm on is bare, the bedding having been removed when Nicole's roommate moved out a few days ago.

"I can bring him back," I repeat. She stares at me. She doesn't understand, couldn't understand what just happened no matter how much I explain to her, and I don't want her to. "All I have to do is text him and say, 'Come back when you're done sending your homework in.' It's that easy."

I fling my legs off the side of the bed and push my hair behind my ears. Even though I'm not looking at Nicole, I can picture her face as she begins to understand what I'm saying. I have no desire for her to discourage me right now, it's why I didn't tell her I was inviting him over when we were baking cookies earlier. I don't want her opinions to influence mine. This has to be my own decision.

I walk through the bathroom and back into my own room. The contrast between the emptiness of Katie's side of the room—or I guess it's not hers anymore—is tremendous to the character that mine still has. Until tomorrow at least.

I straighten one of the origami cranes. I had to stop Katie from taking them down yesterday as she packed. I told her I'd do it myself, that I wanted them up until I left.

I climb up onto my bed as I stare at my phone. I just want more time here, but I won't change my decision to not be here in the fall. I just have to live through this ending. After I've moved out, everything from this year will be only a memory. I'm excited for Scotland, but I'm not sure if I'm ready for things to be really over with Nick.

I look up from my phone as I snap the purple case back on again. Nicole walks in. She has put her long blonde hair up into a pony tail and she stares at me as she sits in the desk chair.

"Did you text him?" she asks.

"Not yet." The snapping of the case onto the phone resounds in the silence.

"He gave you plenty of chances and you didn't make a move. That could tell you something right there. That you didn't, I mean." She pauses. "Do you really want it to end like that? Because if you text him it will."

"I don't know. Eight months, that's how long we've been doing this dance. That's how long it will be until I see him again."

"If you send that text, you know what it means right?" She isn't judging me like I thought she would. She doesn't understand why I'm not excited for Scotland, can't see that I have to get past this ending before that's possible. When I do finally see him again next January, we will both be different people. It won't matter then, I won't know him anymore.

"If you bring him back here, it won't be an insinuation anymore. You'll only be bringing him back for sex."

"I know." I push the button on my phone and the screen lights up.

I send the message and put my phone on the bed next to me. Nicole stands up from the wooden chair and begins to walk back toward her room.

"You don't have to leave. I didn't text what you think."

"What did you say then?"

I stare up at the cranes above my head. Reaching up, I pull on the strand closest to me. There is a soft popping sound as it snaps off the ties from each side of the room.

I look up at the two remaining strands of cranes still strung up, but currently out of my reach. "I told him, 'If I were the girl in your story, I would've turned to look.'"

Sexcapade Sex Fact 9

Despite Avenue Q's assertion that "the Internet is for porn," only 10 to 15% of web searches are for porn, and only 4% of website domains are for porn.

The Silver Bullet
by Joseph Sheldon

Who puts a silver vibrating bullet in their ass? I do. And as I stand here, naked, erect, scared, a tingle of excitement gurgles in my stomach… Or did the knob get stuck?

Shit.

It's the knob.

It shakes, not getting any looser. I pull the spaghetti strand of a wire. Something wriggles loose, but it isn't the bullet. Black covering slips off a red and white wire. What is this? Some analog TV crap? Letting go does not solve the problem and instead of covering back up, the black wire cover sags.

My asshole looks tighter than a Burmese python wrestling a rat. Just as I think it's going to relax, I flex wrong, and the bullet climbs back up into my rectum. Not only can I feel it, I can see it in my standing mirror. Two hairy ass cheeks, one star shaped pecker, and a tail that hangs out and wriggles in the wind. What was I thinking?

At what point did it feel good? How do gay people do this? How do women push things bigger than this out of themselves? My muscles strain. Taffy. They stretch like taffy on a taffy puller, pulling both ways. My sides split open from the pain. I get an inch, move the wrong muscle and back up it goes.

I give the wire a snug tug.

POP.

No.

No. No.

No, no, no. Oh no. No, no. No this cannot be happening. I cannot take a trip to the hospital now. I cannot have this thing removed at the expense of everyone knowing. My mom doesn't even know I'm bisexual, much less sticking things in my butt to see if I'm turned on. Fuck the Christian way of life.

I squint. The damage isn't done. The white wire is still attached. Thank god. Pushing and pulling might work, but that white wire is my last life line. I let go and spread my cheeks for the mirror. Wider? It hurts and flexes the muscles a little more. The bullet can only go so far, but my asshole seems to go on forever. I only wish I was full of shit.

Breathe. Breathe. It's okay, you've got this me. I slip my hand around the cord, rubbing the little white wire just enough to let some slack. Should I pull it like a Band-Aid? Yoink.

GOD NO.

Yeah. Not happening. Relax. One day I'll need to poo. One day when I'm sixty-five and my mom has died disowning me because she thought I was gay. Why is that so bad? Why is that made only worse right now? Why won't this erection die? Why didn't I have enough lotion?

Lotion.

Lotion.

Over the bed, I reach down and grasp the cold plastic with both hands. Holy mother of god this is my saving grace. A few squeezes and lotion drips between the folds. It moves. Cold. Freezing cold. The constant buzzing has become natural to me, as natural as any silver protrusion can be in one's shit hole. Another tug and the walls of my rectum give way. Out it goes, to the middle of the bullet.

There is such a thing as too much lotion. Lotion is everywhere. On my bed, in my hair, there's some on the poster of Cthulhu across the room. My mind explodes from the inside. Just one more tug and I'm finally free. Home free.

The smell stings my nose. Tears drip at the ends of my eyes. It hurts. God it hurts. Thank god my roommates weren't home. The buzzing sounds like it's in the back of my skull, just above my eyes. Straining against the force isn't helping, pulling away has never been so hard. Then, with sudden joy, and excruciating after pain, my rectum is free. Free of it all. Free to spasm uncontrollably as I roll face first into a pile of mixed lotion on the floor.

"You okay in there, bud?" Jordan calls from the other side of the door.

Sexcapade
Sex Fact 10

Between 1980 and 2012, almost 95% of patients with rectal foreign bodies were men. Only about 13% of the total cases in this time required surgical removal.

Examples of the foreign objects found included: tools, vibrators, bottles, balls, fruits, vegetables, light bulbs, candles, and flashlights.

Philosophy and Fugue
by Holly Elliott

The first night you fucked him in a frenzy.
Why is the last time always
the most unsatisfying?
No more mystic shadows on the wall
of your arched back, his hands holding
your upturned hips, his sharp face in profile
timelessly inscribed like the shadows
of the innocent on walls in Hiroshima
captured in the moment, the motion, of death.

You, at least, still see them on the wall,
certain that the strange positional experiments
so wonderfully performed with double joints
are impossible with anyone else.

After the final time,
when you went to his bathroom
to throw away the tampon,
interrupting the moment,
he said he always suspected
this loss of perfection,

Holly Elliott

forgetting the moment you once came
together entirely clothed,
then curled up naked around each other
like a treble clef not before,
but after the music.

A philosopher said once something is named,
it loses innocence.
We never named what we had,
but somehow the innocence wandered.

Last night you dreamed you stabbed his heart
for what he took from you.
Once the word *want* meant not to desire,
but to lack.

One night, you slept on his hand,
the one he used on you. His hand went dead
and in his sleep, he felt it wither, useless,
as he dreamed of nuclear war.

Love in the Time of Collies
by Lisa Lanser Rose

Having sex with a Border Collie in the room is weird sometimes. Nobody wants to have sex with a dog watching. I think it's because you imagine what he's thinking. On the one hand you know he's thinking, "Is it time for Frisbee? Is it time for dinner? Got any rawhide on you?" But you also project your own attitudes and insecurities on him.

That's what dogs are for. For example, I'm neurotic about my weight, so during sex I'm always wondering, do I look fat? And you can't ask the dog. He always says, "Yes. Now make me fat too."

My husband Alby projects completely different thoughts on our Border Collie puppy, Mick. Alby assumes Mick wants everything he wants. He feeds him straight from the table and says, "See? I told you he prefers organic quinoa."

I say, "He prefers organic cat shit too. What's your point?"

But it's the same thing during sex. Alby's convinced Mick wants a piece of me.

Sometimes, when I feel Mick panting on my knee the same way Alby does, it crosses my mind. I know it's impossible for a prepubescent neutered male to look at me and think, "I'd tap that," but it gives me the willies, and not in a good way.

I guess sex got complicated for us back when we started doing the Kama Sutra at the same time we started fostering Border Collies. I want to get an A in Kama Sutra, because that's the kind of worldly overeducated chick I am. I have to keep the manual right there next to us on the porch swing. Then you add the foster dog, and there's no telling *what* they've seen. That first night, Alby and I wrapped around each other, stumbled down the hall, barged into the bedroom, tripped over a squeak toy, fell onto our bed, turned to page forty-three, and began our foray into the Sacred Fog of Intimacy with a foster dog in the room. We were just easing into the Reverse Sherpa when Alby said, "Is she watching?"

I peered over his ankle. She was.

"No," I said. "Besides, she doesn't know what we're doing." Soon she settled on the floor with a chew. We relaxed and managed to ignore, for the most part, the loud slurping sounds she made.

We'd just finished our journey up the Magic Mountain when Alby said, "She didn't bother us once. She's a good dog." Then I saw what had kept her busy—she'd chewed the crotch right out of my panties.

That freaked me out, so when our own Border Collie, Mick, was still a tiny puppy and we grown-ups went upstairs, we left him in his crate downstairs. But that didn't last long, once he discovered yodeling.

Alby's a South African, so he said something like, "Aw, hartseer, arme brakkie. Let's bring him upstairs."

I'm a teacher, so I said, "Mick needs to learn delayed gratification. We don't." But the boys won.

By the time Mick was six months old, foreplay meant wandering the house gathering all the treat-dispensing puzzles. I buy the ones that promise to improve your dog's critical-thinking skills and produce higher scores on standardized obedience tests. We only had about twenty back then.

"How long do you think these'll keep him busy?" Alby said, stuffing soy cheese into the seventh Kong.

I calculated, "Twelve minutes."

Alby winked. "We need more sex toys."

"You mean dog toys."

His first language isn't English, so I cut him some slack.

The first time we let Mick stay in the room, we set him on the floor with his puzzles arranged in a sequence to scaffold Bloom's Taxonomy. Once Mick was completely absorbed in Bob-a-Lot Sudoku, Alby and I attempted the Easy Rider Aardvark, which, as you may know, requires that both of the woman's feet be planted firmly on the floor. (If you buy the twelve-thousand-and-first edition of the Kama Sutra, it comes with these really helpful rubrics you can tape to the mirror so you can grade your performance.) Anyway, from the Aardvark position, a couple can smoothly transition to Piston Bolt Lotus, which is what we were doing when I felt puppy arms wrap around my leg and go tug-tug-tug-tug-tug.

Alby said, "You still think he doesn't understand?"

"He's a puppy," I said. "It's a powergrab."

He said, "Bul kak, I know what kind of grab that was."

I rolled over onto a wet tennis ball. Mick's freckled face panted at the edge of the bed. "Ignore him," I said. A moment later, Mick jumped onto the bed, paced one end to the other, then groaned like a bored teenager and flopped against my back. Alby couldn't stifle his laughter.

"Ignore him," I said. Or I might have just thought it. "Ignore him" had become my silent mantra.

Sometimes, for example, when we're in the Suspended Wombat position, Mick drops his eighteen-inch knotted rawhide bone on my forehead. He investigates every change in my breathing, especially when we're doing the Long-Distance Donkey Trot. I know I should be supportive—I truly believe Mick could be a Respiratory Medical service dog when he grows up. But I lose my patience and swat him away. Now I always need one arm free to fend off the dog. I can't do any of the handstand poses anymore.

The other day, we collected, loaded, and put all the dog puzzles on their "gifted" settings. We even got Grand Theft Auto for Mick's Wii. He loves Chop and all the car-chasing. Mick didn't interrupt us once. We got so absorbed in what we were doing, we never thought about him, not even when we aced the G-Force Square-Peg Town Crier.

Then, we saw what had kept him busy. Mick's puzzles lay untouched, and his back was turned to us. He was in the Slouching Sphinx position and pointed toward the bathroom. When we went to look, we discovered our tabby cat, Audrey, hiding in the sink in the Sulking Tiger position, only her watery green eyes brimming over the rim. Turns out Mick and Audrey can stare at each other like that for hours. Problem solved.

Now whenever Alby's in the mood, he says, "Want to throw the pussy in the sink?" His first language isn't English, so I cut him some slack.

Sexcapade
Sex Fact 11

Participating in yoga has benefits for both men's and women's sex lives. After 12 weeks of yoga, men identified significant improvement with their sexual functioning, while women reported significant increases in sexual arousal, vaginal lubrication, and overall sexual function and satisfaction.

The Killer Whales
by Leah Mueller

Hitchhiking through Illinois on Highway 57 isn't glamorous, even when you're nineteen and restless. The terrain is flat and dull, with cornfields and fast food restaurants like Bob Evans and Long John Silver's. The signs' garish images promise delicious, exciting meals. However, when you wander inside one of the establishments, a surly cashier shoves a plastic basket at you and demands money.

You step into the entryway and find a pay phone. It's dented and filthy, with a long chain dangling limply underneath. Somebody stole the directory, and you'll need to spend a dime to call directory assistance. It's a gamble, paying a stranger to do your research, but you have no choice.

You dial 411 and wait until a nasal voice answers. Breathlessly, you utter Jim's last name. You get lucky, and the operator gives you the correct combination of numbers. Jim's spending the summer with his parents in the tiny, wretched town of Odin. You're fifteen miles away in Marion, not doing much of anything, and wonder if he'd like to see you.

Jim covers the receiver with one hand, asks his mother whether he can borrow the car. He already knows the answer. He's a Geology honors student at Eastern Illinois University, and his parents let him do whatever he wants. You met Jim at Eastern a year ago, before you dropped out. The two of you spent the night on your roommate's couch, alternately fucking and talking about his divorce. He'd impregnated his high school sweetheart a couple of years beforehand. She insisted upon a shotgun wedding, but he left her a few months later. Fortunately, none of this had affected his GPA.

You step into the parking lot and lean against the side of the restaurant. Minutes later, Jim arrives in his parents' station wagon. He doesn't embrace you, but leers at your body instead. "Looking good," he says appreciatively. "Where's your car?"

"I don't have one," you say. "I hitchhiked here. I'm headed north. I happened to be passing through, with occasional automotive assistance."

"Wow," he exclaims. "Where do you live now?"

"New Orleans," you reply, breezily. "What would you like to do?"

"Let's go to a motel," he says, without skipping a beat.

You nod and climb into the passenger seat. Jim places one hand on your thigh, squeezes firmly. He maneuvers the steering wheel and sneaks a peek at your breasts. You're bra-less and wearing a sundress, a look that attracts rides in a matter of seconds. Most of the time, the guys leave you alone, but occasionally you have to ditch the peskier ones at rest stops.

Jim pulls into a motel parking lot and cuts the engine. The blinking sign reads, "Marion Motel: Economical Lodging for Families and Groups." The two of you enter the lobby, and Jim gapes at you nervously. Then he remembers it's 1978, and he doesn't have to pretend the two of you are married. He writes his name on the small white card, and smiles.

The desk clerk accepts Jim's pile of bills, and hands him a plastic key. Inside the room, Jim sticks his hand down the front of your sundress. The two of you kiss, lapping the inside of each others' mouths. Finally, he withdraws and asks, "Are you hungry? I could buy some Big Macs."

You're always hungry, so you nod. Jim returns a half hour later with a bulging, greasy bag. You're stretched out on the bed, watching "Orca, the Killer Whale" on television. "Poor whale," Jim says. "He's just following his biology." He tosses the bag on the mattress. You devour your burger, eyes riveted to the screen. Fishermen with spear guns attack Orca repeatedly. The whale is wily and gives them trouble when they least expect it. He fights furiously, but the men triumph anyway.

Jim switches off the television. He sticks his hands inside your underwear, rubs your clitoris awkwardly with his thumb and forefinger. You're not wet, and it's going to take a while at the rate he's going. You remember him as a better lover, but that was a while ago.

Jim dips his head, goes to work with his mouth. This maneuver is a slight improvement, but his tongue isn't quite in the right place, and you don't know how to tell him. You sway back and forth, hoping it will land in the correct spot. Your tactic doesn't work, and you aren't able to come, even though oral sex is usually a slam-dunk.

Jim stares at you for a moment, unsure of his next move. Finally, he unzips his cutoffs and deposits them on the floor. His dick is skinny and hard. He pushes it into your vagina, thrusts quickly and mechanically, like a jackhammer. After a minute, his body erupts into spasms, and he collapses on top of you.

The room is quiet, except for the distant blast of a truck horn. Jim rises to his feet. "That was a good one," he says with satisfaction. He wanders into the bathroom, then re-emerges, looking refreshed. "I'd better head home now," he says.

You stare at him with disbelief. "You're not spending the night?" you ask. You're not certain why you want him to stay overnight, except it seems like the right thing to do after sex.

Jim shakes his head apologetically. "I can't," he says. "My parents will be pissed. I told them I'd bring the car back in a couple of hours."

You suddenly remember that you're dealing with somebody from an alien world, a person with parents who care about his whereabouts. Jim stares down at your prostrate body with pity. "You shouldn't hitchhike," he says gently. "You should buy a car, like everyone else." He wanders towards the door, pauses for a moment with his hand on the knob. Finally, he steps across the threshold, climbs into his mother's car, and roars across the parking lot towards the interstate. You listen until you can no longer hear the engine.

Sexcapade Sex Fact 12

Gymnophoria is the sense that someone is mentally undressing you, while apodyoposis is the act of mentally undressing someone.

Pretty in Plastic
by Catherine Carson

This was the fifth date. Touching led to kissing. Kissing often led to sex, and social pressure said the third date was the time to get naked, to kiss until lips were chapped, to leave mascara smudges on a pillow case and wake up with messy hair that—God-willing—looked alluring in morning light.

I was two dates late. This was the night.

We were on my couch. My turf. My choice. The machine was in my room, hidden in my nightstand, one drawer below the condoms.

A movie played on my TV, but I was distracted, my hand making the bold and quiet move to his thigh. He didn't flinch, so I looked him in the eyes, his sweet, brown eyes.

What was worse, snoring or putting on the mask? Maybe he would leave after sex.

We kissed slowly. He smelled like cloves.

Him leaving would not be ideal. I needed a tangle of pheromones to tie us together. This man could be forever.

His hands moved to my hair. His fingers cupped my ears.

Maybe I could leave the mask off and he would sleep through my snores.

He pulled me closer. I leaned on his chest.

No, not a chance.

Maybe I would die.

It wasn't too late to call the evening off. But there he was, and his hair was so soft, and I was already unbuttoning his shirt.

Could I put it on after he fell asleep? The noise was white, the hush of a fan. But what if he woke up and screamed, my alien face shocking him in the dark?

I would have to warn him. But not until after sex.

And so I straddled him on the couch. And so we kissed and I pulled off my shirt and led him into my room, the light low and yellow, the sheets soft and pale.

My hands shook. Every minute I got closer to the point of no return, when I would have to put on the mask.

"You are beautiful," he said. He kissed my neck. I turned off the light.

"Are you ready?"

"Yes. I have condoms in my nightstand."

He opened a drawer. There was a hollow zipping sound, the sound of plastic tubing scraping wood.

"Wrong drawer!" I was too late.

"What's this?" he asked, pulling out the entire tube, one excruciating inch at a time. Last, the mask and headgear flopped at the end and banged against the top of the table.

This was it.

"I have something to tell you," I said. "I have sleep apnea. I have to wear a mask. Without it, I snore, and sometimes people die, so I have to wear it. It's not loud. I'll just look a little weird."

These words hung in the air like the mask dangling from his hands.

Then, my great-aunt's voice came to me. "You'd better wear sexy lingerie with that thing," she had said.

The plastic CPAP mask covered my nose and mouth, and its tube was tethered to a black box next to my bed.

It could reach six feet away, sending an arc of air directly into a mouth open in sleep, the same mouth that would release bed-shaking snores without it.

Maybe she was right. Deep, deep breath. I crawled off the bed.

"What are you doing?" he asked.

"This."

From my dresser, I chose my best lingerie: red, with lace against my chest. Gauze fluttered at my hips.

I set my machine on the nightstand and plugged it in. I took the tubing and mask from him and hooked it up. He watched from the bed. I couldn't look at his face.

Then, I pulled the headgear over my hair and snapped it into place. I pushed the button.

I held my breath.

After a second, warm air rushed through plastic and struck my lips. I dropped the strap of my chemise off my right shoulder.

"Now, where were we?" I asked through the mask.

He smiled. "Weren't you getting a condom?"

My smile broke the seal of the mask. I unbuckled it and tore it off my head. The sound whooshed through the room. As deftly as I could, I smacked the button and opened the top drawer, retrieved a condom, and closed the drawer.

When we were done, I waited for him to close his eyes. With my head on his chest, I waited for his heartbeat to slow. Once again, I slipped the mask over my head and snapped on the strap.

I pressed the big button. Even though he'd already seen me in the mask, I curled away from him, wedging the mask between pillow and mattress—tricky, as air still had to escape.

Just when my breathing hit rhythm, his warm hand pressed against my shoulder.

"You're still beautiful," he said.

I closed my eyes, and the room filled with the sweet sound of our breath.

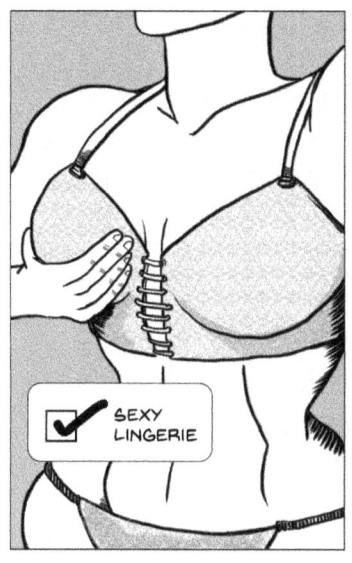
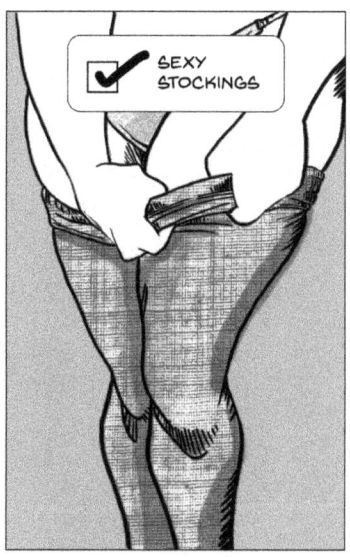
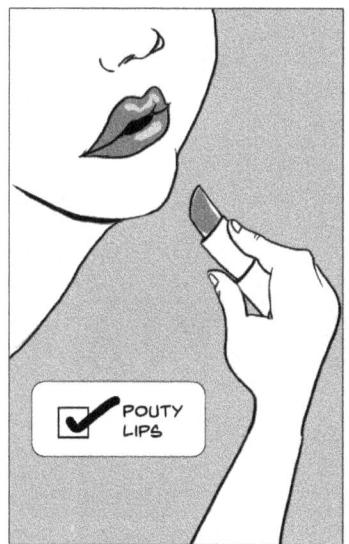

Dress Up Night *BABS! the great*

Sexcapade Sex Fact 13

The length of the vagina expands during arousal. While it may begin around 3 inches long, it can stretch to 5 or more inches as the uterus pulls itself up, making more room for penetration.

Laid Over
by G.B. Lindsey

"Have you ever done this before?" Leo asks.

"No," Jodi—it is Jodi, Leo made a point of remembering this time because, awkward—grunts, tipping into the wall to get her elbow farther down. "If I had, I'd know this was the worst idea ever and wouldn't be doing it again."

Agreed, but Jodi's finally got her fingers where Leo wants them, so Leo spreads her legs as much as she can, tips her head back, and enjoys herself.

Tampering with lavatory smoke detector punishable by law, says the ceiling. "Noted."

"What?"

"Nothing."

"Why Leonida?" Jodi says, tugging fruitlessly at the hem of Leo's skirt. Leo helps her. It's the jean one. It sticks to her legs.

"Mom's a Greek history professor." Somewhere over Greenland, they'd got around to names, brothers and sisters and the requisite stories about Leo's cat. Jodi doesn't have a cat. Jodi's a lizard person. Leo wriggles down onto Jodi's fingers and Jodi gets a hand under her butt to hold her still. Leo's thigh muscles hurt and she has nowhere to put her hands. She tried grabbing onto Jodi's shoulders and they ended up sitting, for lack of a better word, on the toilet lid. The questionably clean toilet lid. "Oh, god. Could you use your thumb?"

"Sure."

"I need leverage." There's a coat hook to the right. Leo fumbles it out of the wall and crooks her ring finger over it. But Jodi presses the pad of her thumb right on the money spot, and Leo yanks down. Okay, that hurts. Coat hooks, bad idea. She flails at the ceiling with both hands and there, there's something she can hold onto—

"Don't mess with the smoke detector!" Jodi hisses.

"Shit, sorry—ow." Funny bone, meet mirror. Leo scrunches her eyes shut, rubbing her elbow. She hopes the door holds. It's a folding one. It took forever to latch. "Ow."

"This is totally sexy."

"Totally sexy."

"It's not working."

"It's totally working, just, okay—" There it comes, tickling up the backs of her thighs. Half a minute at most. How long have they been in here? Is there a line forming outside? Jodi hasn't even gotten off yet. Leo tried eating her out, but that dental dam had been in her purse awhile. Leo couldn't speak to the state of the packaging. And then they would have had to drag Jodi's pants all the way down and when Jodi sat on the sink, her knees got in the way of where Leo would have to be, and besides, crouching on this floor is not something Leo's doing, not with bare knees and, but, "oh, *oh*. Ah." She breathes in and out through her nose, head knocked back against the door, and skates through the tremors. "Okay. Mmm." Wiggles her hips, gets one last jolt. Not mind-blowing, but it'll more than do. "Okay."

Jodi straightens, and Leo spreads her legs again to help Jodi get her hand free. She regains her feet, tugging her underwear up and her skirt down. "Here, turn."

Jodi scoots around, balancing with the heels of her hands on the wall. Leo worms an arm around in front, finds the parted placket of Jodi's pants, and tries to get her hand into her underwear. "Sorry. Elastic's kind of—"

"Yeah." Jodi snaps her underpants up over Leo's wrist, then sighs forward to brace on the wall behind the toilet. Leo gets her other hand up Jodi's shirt, finds her breast, and goes to town.

Jodi's got deep black curly hair, ringlets that would snug around Leo's pinkies. Her nape is brown, two shades lighter than the rest of her. It takes almost two minutes. Leo counts the pretty little spirals of hair as she brings Jodi off, until Jodi's hips jerk, her knees thunk a rhythm on the toilet seat, and then she clenches around Leo's middle finger and hitches against Leo's thumb, and bonks her forehead on the wall.

Leo hisses in sympathy, fumbling her hand free of Jodi's shirt to cup her forehead. "Ouch."

Jodi waves a hand aimlessly. "I've had worse."

They tuck their clothes in and take turns washing their hands at the sink. "Never again," Jodi says.

"Lesson learned." Leo tugs, then kicks at the door. "Won't open."

"Here, let me."

"There's no *room*."

"Stop moving and let—"

The door snaps open and half spills them into the corridor. Luckily the plane's dark and most people are asleep in their seats.

•••

In the airport, Leo uses the bathroom, gets a macchiato, and calls her brother. "Just landed in O'Hare. I'll be home tonight."

"Your cat eats chins."

"Yeah, but you're not using yours."

"Say that to my face."

"I can't, your face makes me vomit."

"Your face is vomit."

"Last call for Flight 643 to San Francisco," says the helpful overhead.

"Ooh, sorry, can't hear you. Places to go."

"Don't forget to read the safety card," says her brother.

"Shut up." It's a superstition. She can't help it.

"I hope you miss your flight," says her brother.

"Then you'd just have to keep feeding your chin to my cat."

"You're a brat. Just like your cat."

"Love you, bye."

"Bye," her brother growl-breathes.

Leo makes it on board and finds her seat. Aisle seat, way in the back. She shoves her purse under the seat in front of her, buckles in, and reads the safety card front to back, then looks over and finds Jodi blinking at her from the window seat.

"Uh."

"Wow," Jodi says. "Going to SF?"

"Yep." Leo fidgets with her seatbelt while they watch the flight attendants wear life jackets and pretend to put oxygen masks over their faces.

The plane takes off. Jodi picks up a magazine.

During the inflight service, Leo gets an orange juice. Jodi declines a drink. Leo sips her juice, and peeks at Jodi, and finds her looking back.

"So. San Francisco?"

Jodi nods. "I live there. Well, not there. In Alameda. I work IT for one of the hospitals."

"That sounds great."

"People need to not click the phishing emails."

Leo slugs back her drink. "I'm going on to San Diego. I'm a teacher. Middle school."

"Lotta flights."

"I like the cheap tickets."

"Mm-hm."

Jodi looks at her. Leo looks back.

Five minutes later, Leo clears her throat, unbuckles, and heads for the lavatory.

•••

"Oh, god. *Oh, god.*"

Jodi rolls her eyes at the ceiling a foot above their heads. "I swear, this girl is praying."

Shirts off this time. Jodi's still not wearing a bra. Her breasts are small and beautiful with wide, hard nipples. Leo has her hands all over them.

Jodi shakes her head, thumbing Leo's nipple through lace. Leo's way too big to ever go without a bra. Too much back pain. "Girl, you are really wet."

"Well," Leo huffs, and uses Jodi's shoulder to hitch herself higher. "My vagina really likes you."

Jodi pushes her face between Leo's and hums against her sternum. It tickles.

"That's interesting," Leo offers.

"Not doing it for you?"

Leo has no idea. Maybe if she weren't in an airplane lavatory.

"At least," Jodi whispers loudly, "we don't have to worry about dicks."

"This is the most romantic conversation I've ever had with someone's fingers up my vagina."

Jodi has a snorty laugh. "You talk about your vagina a lot."

"My vagina and I have a great relationship today."

Jodi cracks right up, a bright cackle, and then Leo's giggling too and they fall into the sink. Someone's elbow knocks the faucet, spraying water all over them. That's about the time the flight attendant hammers on the door.

"Stop banging," Jodi calls.

"You stop banging!" the flight attendant yells back.

•••

"Well."

"I have never been kicked off an entire airline before," Jodi says.

At least she's already home. Leo sighs and gets out her phone.

"No," answers her brother.

"What are your thoughts about feeding my cat again?"

"Seriously. You missed your flight?"

Yes, that's what they're calling it these days. "They overbooked."

"So, what, they're pushing you onto the next flight?"

"No…" Leo tries to turn the volume down but her brother is just loud. "No, those are all full."

Jodi laughs at her.

"Who's that?"

"Another passenger. Listen, I can't fly out until tomorrow, can you just drop by one more time and—"

"Sure. You okay? You have a place to stay?"

Jodi signals her with both hands: two enthusiastic thumbs up. Leo frowns. "Uh, yes?"

"We'll get her a room in Alameda," Jodi yells at the phone. A family of five stops their luggage train to look. Leo turns away. Jodi follows her. "Bed and breakfast. Turn down service!"

"Who *is* that?"

"No one, anyway, thank you so much, the cat loves you. Really. I have to go."

"To Alameda?"

"Bye." Leo hangs up. "Thanks. Thank you. A lot."

"You're welcome," Jodi says. "Come on."

Leo fingers the strap on her purse. "You don't have to do that."

"I like my luck in threes."

•••

Jodi fishes a new dam out of a kitchen drawer with spatulas in it and goes down on Leo—"Jeez, freckles there, too?"—in the hallway under the Ikea sconce. Her bed is lush, a king-size. She lights a bunch of candles, but then the room stinks like piña colada, so they put them out and open the windows. Jodi performs a striptease and trips over a pair of nylons on the floor, then lobs a condom at Leo's head "so you don't impregnate me." Leo laughs so hard she farts.

But the sex is great.

Play Through The Pain
by C.C. Reed

The lighting is poor and there is no cheesy soundtrack. We don't have clever stage names like, Poppy DeCherry and Jack Hammer. No surgically endowed extra waits in the wings to step into the shot in case of equipment failure, because real sex is not like a porno movie.

Sex is more like a sporting event. In real life, when real bodies engage in real sport, there is a real possibility that one of the athletes will cramp up and keel over. Because I'm middle-aged, I sometimes skip foreplay to do gentle stretching exercises instead.

Staying 'warmed up' 24/7 may be the secret to a long-lasting marriage, but sports injuries can happen even if a person has done proper warm ups. If a middle-aged wife and her middle-aged spouse take a joy ride on an All Terrain Vehicle, as the rhythm, speed and intensity of the ride increase, so does the potential for injury. Even if the ATV is parked in the middle of a cornfield, and the engine is no longer running, and the lights are off, injuries can occur. If she is warmed up and he has his lights on, when spine repeatedly meets roll bar on the back of an ATV, sports injuries happen.

Real life, every day, run-of-the-mill injury, can further elevate the risk of sport injury.

In a porn film, Jack wouldn't slip a disk while doing a happy dance, having just finished the job of shoveling a ton of limestone gravel around the calf hutches at his farm. Poppy wouldn't break her wrist as she wrestled with a jammed switch on an emergency spotlight. But, if Jack and Poppy were real middle-aged athletes, in a real sporting event, they would have to play through their pain.

Because of his back injury and her broken wrist, Poppy and Jack hadn't spent any quality time together between the sheets in more than a week. The couple measured sexual frequency in dog years, so a day was actually a week and a week was seven months, or seven years or, oh hell. They were horny and hurting so they brought in reinforcements. Big Boy, the vibrator joined them for an evening of fun and games.

Santana music played in the background. Candlelight danced across the ceiling. Warm, sweet flesh on crisp linen promised a wonderful time, but something was off.

"Big Boy needs lubricant" Poppy said.

"Already used some."

No, something was not right. "Try some more."

Spritz, spritz, spray, spritz. Carlos teased the guitar strings. Drum rhythm quickened.

"Yes. That's better. But. But, *we don't have any SPRAY lubricant! What IS that!?*"

"I don't know. It's lubri… It's, I can't read it without my glasses!" He flipped over to show her the bottle in the dimly lit room and laid his full body weight on her broken wrist. She screamed in pain. Startled, Jack jerked sideways and threw his back out again.

"Sorry honey." Jack moaned, "It was this. This is, oh my God! I'm so sorry. Are you all right? Are you all?"

<u>Snore No More</u>! Peppermint oil spray to numb the back of the throat so the soft palate doesn't vibrate as you wander dreamland! Peppermint cools and numbs soft tissue.

By God, it did just that!

He couldn't move. Her wrist (not even close to the target area) throbbed. Big Boy hummed and gyrated in a happy little circle around the middle of the bed. Jack lay writhing in pain as Poppy made a bowlegged-cowboy-dash for the stairs. Holding her thighs apart, she teetered into the bathroom. Numb from bum to belly button, she felt only the unprecedented urge to douche with Drano or Lime Away or some toxic chemical that might restore any sensation to her, definitely not vibrating, soft tissue.

She took an emergency shower. She thought about the true athletes who play through their pain. *Never quit. It's not over til it's over. No pain no gain.*

She thought about her sister Vickie, whose trip to the emergency room after an evening of fun and games, (when she wrenched her knee on the dismount) could serve as inspiration to any Olympian. If mild-mannered Vickie could play through the pain, with Kerri Strug's Olympic spirit and style, (arms extended - all of her weight on one foot) the wild-mannered little sister could try. *Try again. If you snooze you lose, so snore no more!*

With my good hand, I grabbed (I mean ah, Poppy grabbed) a pair of reading glasses, a flashlight, some soothing lotion, and then ran back upstairs. The Santana CD started over.

There was no improvement in the lighting, but the soundtrack was great.

Condoms and Hot Tubs Don't Mix

Francisco
by Gemma Cooper-Novack

Will you go down on me?

my words
rose on steam over the marble floors that kept
    my empty
room inside the archway
overlooking
the dark of the Midway, the coming spring
        then

he was everywhere on the bed above
and below me   extralong
twin sheets crumpling
and forgetting and against
my clitoris he whispered *this is your clitoris*

(maybe I should have gotten up then but it would
have been precarious and anyway I knew
it was my clitoris like I knew it was Malaysia on
    a map
it wasn't as if I'd actually been there)

I said *I know*
and he nodded into it

and I didn't know I had that many senses that many
branches everywhere I didn't know these ricochets
               and the window
tilted I was smack
against the Midway tilting the thoroughfare majestic
white buildings of history replacing the whites of my
               eyes the whites of
my thighs he was
curly against skin that had never occurred to me

stop

and instantly

the mattress hung in the air and
he was leaning
into my ear *just so you know*
he said *I'm pretty good at that*
so if you're ever with anyone else
and it feels different …

(maybe I should have gotten up then
but it was my room and impossible
               I'd been watching
the light in his window for weeks across the courtyard)

Condoms and Hot Tubs Don't Mix

that had all felt different enough to me anyway
couldn't anything for a while hold still?

he didn't
stay when the room righted and it wasn't for a second
because I hadn't asked   so I didn't
get up when he left
just watched
with one eye open as the door
swung shut

Sexcapade
Sex Fact 14

Injuries sustained during sex are more common than reported, partially because of the reporting party's embarrassment, and partially because the body's tolerance for pain increases during sex, and many people don't notice they've been injured until after sex is over.

Getting Lewd on Ludes
by Jim Ross

I love how Halloween grants us license to surrender to the shadow and metamorphose into someone or something we're not. But, that particular Halloween night—in a group house we self-consciously called a commune—Halloween wasn't working for me. In the corner by the vestibule door, under the coatrack's mushrooming canopy, a yellow-green caterpillar wound herself around Frankenstein and his amiable, though overly mascaraed bride. Beneath our porcelain dining room table, a devil whose horns flickered like tiny Christmas trees put the moves on a priest dressed in white collar, black velvet dress, and long blonde locks. Joan of Arc valiantly tried to mount her unsteady steed on the living room's orange Herculon couch.

Among those engaged in verbal forms of communication, people spat words at each other simultaneously, abruptly paused to digest, then spat out reactions simultaneously, paused abruptly again to digest, over and over, like crows feeding each other. It looked like a fencing match in which both parties periodically froze.

Convulsions of laughter, punctuated by fits of silence, burst from the space without a name. The laughter seemed to possess them. Not knowing why they laughed, but feeling they knowingly embraced chaos, strained me.

I put my hand on housemate Antoni's head as his laughter reached a fever pitch. He said, "I'm only laughing," and smiled.

I asked housemate Carol, "Doesn't he suffer from the laughter?"

She lifted her left hand and slowly crossed its pointing finger over her middle finger of the right hand.

"Does the pointing finger represent suffering? And the middle finger, laughter?" I asked.

"That's what it is—the suffering and the laughing—together," said Carol, rubbing her two fingers across each other.

I turned to Antoni and asked, "Isn't it a strain?"

Antoni replied, "Not if you laugh in, but most people laugh out."

I returned to my kitchen space. When the laughter ceased, I wondered, had they all left? Had they morphed? I fluttered back to where I saw them last. Antoni played zither, while partygoer Peter strummed guitar. Peter led. Now and then, he spat out words, such as, "Someone ought to pay me for something," or "It's not coming natural," or "They allow me two cups of steam a day," or, "Is everything singular or plural?"

Then he started laughing, "I just remembered who I am." And then they all laughed together. In.

I felt out of place, but couldn't come up with the right simile. Once I did, I could sneak out and go to bed. What about, like a stinkbug running errands in a perfume factory? No, *I don't stink*. Like a lightening bug trying to ignite micro-summers in dead of winter? Not quite, but it bestows warmth and suggests summer will roll around again. What about: like an albino ant marooned on a raft that's going up in flames and on the brink of sinking below the waterline? Ha, that taps into my fear of shadowy figures infiltrating my home. Wait, one more: like a porcupine turning cartwheels at a balloon party? Trivial, perhaps, but it captures my party-spoiler reputation, as someone who says, "Grow up. It's not okay."

Convinced the right simile will find me, I began to secret my way up our oak staircase. Two reddish monkeys wearing identical blue and white polka-dotted aprons played poker on the quarter landing, their legs outstretched like an impromptu obstacle course. At stair head, a crowd sang Stephen Stills' *Love the One You're With* behind closed bathroom doors. I held my breath and tip-toed by, fell into my bedroom door, and dove for my bed well before witching hour.

Still smeared with whiteface—my last-resort, half-hearted Halloween costume—I snapped into sleep. Doorknob rattling startled me. Someone barefoot or sock-wearing padded across the thickly carpeted floor.

A female voice whispered, "You mind if we use your room for 30 minutes?" In dreamy logic, I figured the question was a come-on within a dream. I chose to move onto another dream rather than entertain the question. Within seconds, there was motion on the floor alongside my bed. So, it *wasn't* a dream after all! What now? Eyes glued shut, my ears stayed wide open. Sham sleep became my Halloween mask.

"I don't know how," a second female voice said.

"I'll show you," said the first female voice.

"I can't believe this," said the second voice.

"Believe it."

"There's someone else here," the second voice said.

"Ignore it."

"Slower. Slower," said the second voice.

"You just tell me. Whatever you want."

It sounded like someone was enjoying a dark chocolate mousse. I held onto that image.

"My mother'd kick you," laughed the second voice.

"I'll hold you."

"It's cold in here," said the second voice.

"You're feeling warmer already."

"Poor Richard," the second voice lamented.

"Only think about you."

"I threw up," said the second voice.

"You've been spitting a lot. It'll pass."

Pause.

"Funny, I feel less guilty now," said the second voice.

"You said you couldn't handle it. That's how I knew

you'd be interested."

Another pause.

"Should we go back?" asked the second voice.

"The party's here. The party's us."

"We better go," said the second voice.

There was a flurry. Like pheasants rising from marshy grasses, they rose without even a whisper. After soft baby steps, my door fanned open. Hallway light slapped me across the face. Then faster than it had opened my door fanned shut, sending a welcome breeze, as if feathers brushed my face. The cylinder of the door handle faintly ground. Then the latch bolt ejected firmly through the strike plate, with the finality of gunshot. Good cat burglars, except for the gunshot.

I didn't feel much like drifting back into sleep. I rose, found the door, barefooted out into the harsh light, made my way around the latest staircase adventurers, and looked around for two women who'd cut themselves off from the melee. I found two women sitting on the Herculon couch, holding hands pretzel-like, with the far hands clasped over the near. Focused on each other, neither said a word. I joined them on their couch, not too close. Their eyes briefly settled on my whiteface. Did they recognize me? After ten minutes of shared equanimity, I rolled into a standing position, bowed, navigated the stairway, embraced my bed, and slept until the sun jolted me bolt upright.

•••

My six housemates were undergrads at a university northwest Washington, DC. I was a grad student at another university across town. I'd moved into the basement in January because a friend who knew "a commune member" invited me along to the house's Christmas party. For the first five months, my housemates told me they welcomed my "more mature, reasoned perspective." Then in June—after three of the four founders of the house graduated and moved out, but before three new arrivals moved in—I was offered the big bedroom upstairs, where the sun first shows her face every morning. The newly-reconfigured house members were more likely to tell me to "get over it and get with it." A late Victorian with wrap-around porches, the house's owner was a widow who drank. Renting to students amused her.

•••

When I came downstairs the morning after, I had the house to myself—not counting the three dogs—for nearly three hours. None of the dogs were mine, but I began my morning chores—cleaning up where the dogs shat in the living room, dining room, kitchen, and the wide open space with no name. When I'd finished shit patrol, I fetched the *Washington Post*, and made myself comfortable in the wicker rocker on the wraparound porch beneath my bedroom, still the beneficiary of the early morning's direct sun.

Around eleven, I heard tumblers on the stairway in search of coffee and OJ. From fragments of conversation I overheard on the porch, there'd been lots of hookups last night, but none of it made sense. Aside from the usual heavily-laced marijuana, there'd been a Halloween treat. Quaaludes (aka: Ludes or Sopors) had been doled out like candycorn. I hadn't noticed.

"Oh, what a marvelous bunch of coconuts!" housemate Dan exclaimed. He, Kate and Antoni stood in the wraparound porch's doorway hand-in-hand.

Dan stepped onto the porch and whispered, "What'd you do last night?"

"I went to bed," I said.

"With who?" he asked.

"With me," I answered.

"There really wasn't anybody with you?" Dan asked.

"Methinks you know the answer. A couple of women came in after I'd fallen asleep," I said. "Asked if they could use my room. I feigned sleep. They did their thing and left."

"And you didn't join them?" Dan asked.

"What was going on was complicated enough."

"There's nothing wrong with a third person jumping in," Dan said.

"As it is, they had Poor Richard to deal with," I said.

"Richard?" Dan asked.

"Yes, that's what she called him. 'Poor Richard.' I guess she and Richard are partners, except on Halloween," I said.

"Hmmm. What were you thinking about while this was going on?" Dan asked.

"A really rich, dark cholate mousse," I said. "Lip-smacking good."

"I can't believe you didn't join them," he said. "What are ludes for?"

"I didn't take ludes or drop them or whatever the hell it is you do with them. And nobody told me our Halloween party was a Quaalude Party," I said.

"You disapprove?" Dan asked.

"I love dark chocolate mousse, if that's what you mean," I said.

Dan turned and walked back into the dining room. I followed. Shortly, tiny housemate Anne came down holding hands with partygoer Marcie. Anne's towering boyfriend, Mark the carpenter, the one with the mountain-man beard, hadn't shown up for last night's bash.

"They got lewd on ludes," said Dan.

Anne turned her head away, looking simultaneously shy and excited.

Gradually, the magnitude of last night's Quaalude orgy began to sink in. People had hooked up randomly and in multiples. Kate, a committed straight with a long-standing boyfriend, Paul, back home in Rhode Island, had hooked up with straight partygoer Mary. Lifelong gay partygoer Peter had hooked up with lifelong straight Carol.

"I've been wanting to get pregnant so I could have a baby" said Peter, as he followed Carol from kitchen to dining room to living room. "It shouldn't always have to be the woman's burden. Now I don't know what to think."

"I've got to call Paul," Kate said. "He needs to come out too. Once he comes out, all of this will be okay, and he and I can still be together . . . when we're together."

"We're all bodies. It's all the same, male or female. It really doesn't matter, sex or no sex. A body is a body," said Antoni, a lifelong gay who regularly smoked marijuana with his mother and had multiple hookups last night, at least two men and one woman.

Anne sat at the dining room table holding hands with Marcie.

"Now I'm dealing with my latent homosexuality," said Bill, a lifelong gay housemate who'd hooked up with a lifelong gay partygoer last night. "Later, I'll deal with my latent heterosexuality."

"Janet and Mariann hooked up last night too," said Dan.

So, Dan *did* know about my midnight visitors.

As the worm turns, Dan turned and asked me, "You want to tell us about *your* night?"

"Sorry, I've been up for hours, I've cleaned up after the dogs, cleaned up after your bacchanal, and I'm late for my run. We can pick up on this later," I said, leaving the prunes to stew in their juices.

The rest of the day was relatively quiet because my nocturnal housemates napped for most of it. When we crossed paths, I listened, smiled, and asked "D'you enjoy it?" After they said something approximating "yes," I typically asked, "Does all this make sense to you?" Their most articulate response was, "Nothing makes any sense anyway, so why not?"

•••

The next day, I rode the H-2 bus to the DC public high school where I was substitute teaching in social studies and then attended a grad school seminar, while my housemates did their earnest best to attend classes. With their central nervous systems still acutely depressed, their scholarly efforts demonstrated the difference between attending classes and being attentive in class. After a makeshift dinner—everyone doing their own thing, meaning a slice of American cheese with a coke and nachos for all of them except Anne—the time approached for our regular Monday night house meeting.

When we'd all gathered in the living room, the doorbell rang. Kate pranced to the door and led Mariann and Poor Richard into the living room. Nobody said who'd invited them, but I guessed it had been Kate's doing. Still, their disruption offered a welcome diversion from the prospect of regaling Saturday night's Quaalude Party and celebrating every coming out.

By "coming out," they had a specific, divergent meaning. Coming out really meant, "crossing over." Crossovers from straight to gay, from gay to straight, from either to ambivalent or simply queer, were celebrated as if a new child had been born. Hours of arguments often followed about who really had sex with whom and whether there was a true crossover.

Apparently, Mariann had beseeched Richard to move into our vacant basement. At Kate's direction, Mariann and Richard—who rented an apartment together—explained their hopes and dreams as prospective new "commune members." Dan, who'd been twitching like never before, switched into full-on tsunami mode.

"Does Richard know what happened here Saturday night?" Dan asked.

When he got no response, Dan pressed harder: "Look at me, Mariann. Does Richard know?"

Poor Richard looked at Mariann. "What the hell's he talking about?" he asked as fear welled up in his eyes.

Mariann didn't answer Dan. She didn't look at Richard. Instead, her eyes threw poison darts at Dan. Then she turned toward Kate with sorry eyes that begged for a life raft.

"You two really need to leave and talk," said Dan.

"Why are you being so brutal?" asked Kate, shaking her fist at Dan.

"Maybe we better go," said Mariann. She sprung from her seat, pivoted, and progressed toward the door without looking back. Poor Richard followed. Kate ran after Richard.

Once Poor Richard and Mariann had driven away, Kate ran back into the house and, still standing, and pointed a finger at Dan, "Why'd you do that?"

"It wouldn't be fair to them or us. This house is coming together. Having them move in might ruin their relationship. Even worse, dealing with their relationship would definitely stifle the energy that's growing in this house," Dan said.

"People can change," said Anne, meekly.

"I admit, we need to talk about where we're headed as a group," said Kate.

"Things have changed," said Dan.

"But did they really change that much?" asked Carol.

"Not really. I still clean up the dog shit every morning," I said.

"You're not obliged to," said Antoni. "That's your choice. You could leave the dog shit right where it is and eventually someone might start picking it up. You haven't given it a fair chance. If you wait long enough, it might even pick itself up."

"That's not what we need to talk about," said Dan. "Something's going on. It's affecting all of us. Or nearly all."

"We're all affected," said Anne. "You can't force change on people. Acceptance is change too. Accepting surprises in ourselves but also accepting differences in others."

"Regardless," said Dan, "We've learned something. Some of us thought we were straight. Some of us thought we were gay. We've learned sexuality is more fluid than that."

"Meaning what?" asked Anne.

"I don't have to avoid having sex with someone because of their gender, but that doesn't mean I have to feel attracted to *everyone*. I don't have to have sex with *everyone*," said Antoni

"Unless you're on sopors," interjected Bill.

"Oh, we're all whores," said Kate. "I need to call Paul and fix this."

•••

Over the next two months, I walked on fiery nails. Every word I spoke placed me at risk of being subjected to a radical sexual analysis. I feared one day I would suck in all the air for a mile around, blow it out all at once, and curse the day.

With no savings and living on a meager substitute's income, I couldn't readily move out. Instead, nearly every Friday, I took the slow train to New York, where I stayed with either Laurie or Elaine, whoever'd have me. I rode the train back to DC on Monday. That gave me three or four days for substitute teaching. I fantasized leaving the whole DC scene behind and moving to New York. I imagined living at the Metropolitan Museum of Art. But grad school kept me in DC and living in New York required real money, which I didn't have.

By staying away most weekends, I avoided the Saturday Quaalude parties and the Sunday regaling. I couldn't escape the week-long efforts to reconcile conflicting reports about Saturday night's goings on and the assignment of Apgar scores to each afterbirth.

Kate and Paul broke up during his next visit after she insisted he "come out" so they could be equals. She falsely claimed she dumped him because they were no longer equals.

When I returned from New York around dinner time one late November Monday, I discovered a crude drawing of a house on the kitchen blackboard. "Come out PLEASE!" was written scribbled above the drawing. An arrow pointed to my room.

Our weekly house meetings were getting even more tiresome. "You know," said Dan, pointing a finger at me at one of those meetings, "lots of energy has been spent on you for no response."

I turned to Antoni and said, "I heard I'm regressing."

Antoni said, "We're all regressing."

Bill said, "Hey, look, it's no joke. Being gay's a serious thing."

"This house has direction now and you can't flow with it," said Kate.

"Kate's undergone astounding changes in emotions so rapidly," said Dan. "She needs another gay woman to support her."

"You never totally lose interest in a sex to which you were attracted," said Bill, "but Kate wants to turn mostly to women."

"You're right," I said. "This house has new energy and a new identity and I don't fit. This isn't the house I moved into in January. You better believe I want to get the hell out of here. I'm exploring my options."

•••

A few days later, I fell asleep with my back facing my bedroom door. I woke when I sensed a hand resting on my right hip. Warm flesh pressed against mine from behind. Fingernails dug into my hip. My first thought was that Jeanne, who still had a key, decided to pay me a surprise visit. I turned to my right and saw Dan's mustached, vapid face shared my pillow. I reared back and swung a sharp right elbow into his chest as if I swung for the right field fences. I followed through by using my open left palm to send him flying. A cry broke from his lips as he looked for the rip cord on his parachute. It sounded like he landed twice. After drawing in a quick breath, he whimpered, "What'd you do that for?" Then he stood and, as he left, said, "I was only trying to help." He paused after each word for full effect.

I let out a roar. I let the silence sink in and roared again and then again. Nobody came to ask why I roared in a dark room at midnight. After nobody came, I hoped I hadn't woken anyone because I didn't want to explain what happened, and didn't happen. I knew Dan was awake so at least he heard me. I pushed the door shut until the latch bolt ejected firmly, with the finality of gunshot.

•••

At daybreak, I walked to Heckinger's Hardware and purchased a chain lock. Screwing it into the doorframe and the door before anyone else was even awake gave me a modicum of satisfaction, but didn't damper my fear-riddled fury.

I phoned one of the former house residents—one of the founders of the original "commune," who'd moved out in June—about moving in with him on a temporary basis ASAP. He said January was the earliest he could arrange.

After I got home from work, the house sounded empty, so I went down to the basement to put clothes in the washer. I was startled to find Anne there. She was the only housemate I still respected and trusted. She, Mark, and I had gone raspberry picking in Rock Creek back in June. We'd enjoyed concocting vegetarian dinners together prior to the recent Quaalude craze.

"What was that noise last night?" she asked. Her attic room was directly above mine.

I told her what happened.

"What was Dan thinking?" she asked. "You've drawn the line very clearly. He had no business... I'm sorry." She dropped her basket of clean laundry and held me. "I'm not happy here either. I'm working on getting out."

"Me too," I said.

"What're you going to do?" she asked.

"Get back on track. Find a place where I belong," I said.

When the crew arrived home, Dan called for an emergency house meeting at 7:30 by writing it on the kitchen blackboard. He also wrote: "Jim placed a lock on his bedroom door, against house policy."

I showed up in the living room last to avoid having to recapitulate for latecomers. I looked around and saw a friend in Anne's eyes. I sat next to Kate, at the end of the Herculon couch. "Are we here because I put a lock on my bedroom door and that's against house policy?"

"Yes," said Dan, looking around for support.

"Well, I admit, I did that," I said. "And I put the lock on my bedroom door because it's no longer safe for me to sleep without one after last night."

"What happened last night?" asked Anne, knowing the answer.

"Dan entered my room in the middle of the night, long after everyone was asleep. While I slept, he got into *my* bed, naked. He put his hand on *my* hip and pressed his flesh against *mine*. All uninvited."

"Did that really happen, Dan?" asked Kate. "D'you really do that?"

"That's . . . that's true," Dan said.

"But why, Dan? Hasn't Jim drawn the line clearly enough?" asked Anne.

"I was only trying to help," Dan answered. "Everyone else has succeeded in coming out. I thought Jim needed a little help. A nudge."

Staring Dan down with the eyes of a tiger, Anne asked, "Are you out of your mind?"

"These days, what does it mean to be in our right minds?" Dan asked.

"You've lost it!" Anne said.

Dan pulled up his t-shirt and pointed at his sternum. "You see this bruise? Jim did this."

"And you know *why* I shoved you out of my bed?" I asked.

"You hurt me. On purpose," Dan said. "We can't have willful violence in this house."

"You imply you think I was wrong to defend myself. You know what? I'm not dignifying this," I said. "You entered *my* bed unwanted. I threw you out of *my* bed. I'm entitled. So are all of you every time someone violates your bed, ludes or no ludes."

"But can't anyone understand, I was only trying to help?" Dan pleaded.

"You were wrong, Dan," said Anne.

"This is so fucked. Jim let you off easy," said Kate.

"What if it'd been me?" asked Carol.

"It would've been different if Jim and Dan had both been, like, luded out and said 'Yeah, let's get it on,'" Antonio said.

"There's no such a thing as consent when you're on ludes," Anne said. "Ludes kill the capacity for consent. They turn us into sick monkeys doing experiments on each other."

•••

The next week, Kate went to the free VD clinic and confirmed she had gonorrhea and crabs. Acting like players in an Arlo Guthrie song, Kate led her housemates down to the VD clinic together, hand in hand, so they could turn the other cheek in succession. Soon, they were all taking penicillin, trimming pubic hair, and bathing in Kwell. More Kwell could be found in our bathrooms than milk in the fridge. After all, I was the only one buying milk and the only one not bathing in Kwell. In addition to the lock on my bedroom door, I began putting a combination lock on my milk carton.

Matters escalated when housemate Bill came down with The Great Pox. The next day, a scribbled note was posted on the fridge door:

What to do during VD Starvation Week
1. watch TV
2. take long shits
3. eat, eat, eat (avoid spicy foods)
4. take sopors
5. dance (but not to the point of arousal)
6. visit in large groups with hands tied
7. read National Geographic
8. tease the opposite sex
9. throw Christmas tree bulbs at passing cars
10. make movies rated G

Despite #4, ingestion of Quaaludes took a downturn. In addition to Anne's comment about ludes turning people into sick monkeys, my housemates had been lectured at the Free VD Clinic about Quaalude risks: destroying the central nervous system; wrecking kidneys, liver, and other vital organs; and interfering with brain function and *ability to take finals*. They'd already purchased Quaaludes by the bottleful so instead of ceasing they opted to use "with greater discretion." Dan still maintained ludes were aphrodisiacs. From everything I read, Quaaludes were a muscle relaxant and hypnotic, which (according to *Time Magazine*) strongly impaired the "conscience muscle."

•••

On a long New York trip over Christmas break, I got to take some long, deep breaths. I cooked up a storm and threw a party at a friend's apartment for people drawn from different parts of my life, some of whom had never met each other before. I walked on the cold sand at Jones Beach. I confirmed that in mid-January I'd be able to move in temporarily with one of the original founders of the house while I looked for more permanent lodging.

When I returned to DC, I learned Mariann was pregnant with Poor Richard's child. To avoid flunking out, Antoni dropped out for the semester before leaving to smoke weed with his widowed mother.

•••

One of my last nights in the house, five of my six housemates sat in a crescent moon on the living room floor smoking marijuana laced with hallucinogens. Dan proclaimed, "Six happy vegetables: a tragicomedy staged in five acts simultaneously on one bed."

"I want to be a tomato," said Kate. "Oh, no, I can't. That has sexist connotations. I'll be a carrot."

"Then I'll be a tomato," said Antoni.

"I'll be a cabbage," said Bill.

"Mariann wanted to be a cabbage too," said Kate.

"Who wants to be a hot potato?" asked Carol.

"Six happy vegetables, nourished by nicotine and sopors," cried Antoni.

•••

The day I left, whatever the dogs vomited yesterday on the stairway was dried and flaking. Raisins scattered on the floors had hardened into wrinkly marbles. Heaps of dog shit everywhere had turned white and lost any hint of stink. Every pan and pot—in the sink or cabinets—wore remains of the meals long past. There was no milk in the fridge, no cheese, not even diet coke. Dishes were shelved randomly, e.g., lunch plate over teacup over soup bowl. "Whatever" was the ruling principle.

I regretted giving up my bedroom where the sun tossed me out of bed and the wraparound porch where I rocked my way through the sunrise edition of the *Washington Post* in peace. But I was free now, like a journalist who'd visited a looney bin—where cannibals held him captive, cross-questioned him hourly, and incessantly sang the Partridge Family's *I Think I Love You*—and finally escaped on a postal truck (the original meaning of "going postal."). Like a lightning bug who took a flying leap from a kid's jar on a summer's day. Like that albino ant who airlifted to safety before the rapids devoured his fiery raft. And, most of all, like that porcupine who could turn cartwheels whenever the spirit moved without fear of reprisals for bursting someone's balloons.

•••

Five months later, after I'd been in a third story walk-up on my own for a couple of months, I looked out my bedroom window one morning. A flight below, across the alley, I saw tiny Anne hanging a planter filled with pink and white gardenias from a beam above the green-painted, wooden balcony at the back of an old brownstone.

"Hey, neighbor!" I called out.

Anne looked up, "Hiya, neighbor! Ha! You live there?"

"Yeah, you?" I asked.

"Yeah," Anne said. "How long you lived there?"

"Two months," I said. "You?"

"Two days, me and Marcie" said Anne, laughing. "We haven't even started unpacking, but I had to make this balcony mine. I could've used your help reaching this beam."

I said, "I hear the raspberries are asking to be picked."

Love is in the Air *BABS! the great*

Sexcapade Sex Fact 15

Penile fractures can occur when an erect penis experiences a force that creates a snapping or popping sound. Surgery is usually necessary to remedy this painful injury.

What You Finally Attend To
by Chelsey Clammer

You are fully aware of the fact that you are a lesbian. You are fully aware of the fact that he is a straight man. And you are fully aware of the fact that your underwear is sopping wet right now because you are thinking about him. This has been going on for nine years.

But during those nine years you were a lesbian and he was a straight man and you had a crush on him but there was that whole lesbian/straight man dynamic thing going on so what could you do? You shrugged your shoulders. And yet your body and your wants persisted. The fantasies you couldn't fight. How they pressed on your skin, surged through your blood, unable for you to ignore.

Nine years go by.

And then it is February 2012, and the two of you start up a conversation about erotica on Facebook. Thank you social media website.

The two of you talk.

By the end of that seven-hour long talk, you, the lesbian, have told him about the crush you have always had on him, and he, the straight dude, has told you about the crush he has always had on you, and you have chatted about fucking each other and you have taken a few masturbating breaks and by the end of it all he has purchased bus tickets and in two weeks will take a 26-hour bus ride to come see you.

He takes a 26-hour bus ride to come see you.

And then he comes.

And then you come.

And then he raises up his head and he says, *God I love eating pussy!*

And then you say, *Me too!*

And then you, the lesbian, are dating a man.

And as you date this man, you are fully aware of yourself, of how you have finally attended to your sopping wet underwear.

You inform your mother of this radical shift in your sexuality. She is a bit shocked. She has always liked your girlfriends, always accepted you for who you are. And so this time around, when there is another flip in your sexuality, she's the one that says, "It doesn't matter what gender the other person is as long as you love them," which is the exact same thing you said to her twelve years ago when you first declared yourself a lesbian.

You as a lesbian: the girlfriends, the gay bars, the one night stands with softball dykes, the crushes on coaches, the picking of pubes from teeth, the way you drool at women who smoke cigarettes. Twelve years of picking pubes. Twelve years of drooling. Yes. Lesbian.

But now there is a man inside you. A man who is your best friend, who is your only male friend, who is the only man you would ever let slip himself inside of you. This, in a way, is what you have been waiting for. The dildos did a fantastic job, but there was always that nagging feeling of wanting something more.

Perhaps it was that something about him that nagged at you for that something more.

Funny story: You wouldn't have met him had it not been for your lesbianism. You were a senior in high school and didn't know where to go to college, so you asked your boss, who you had a crush on, what to do. She told you to apply to her alma mater. You loved her so much, wanted her so much that you would do anything to make her happy, to make her approve of you, and hopefully like you and perhaps have sex with you, so of course you didn't say no. You applied. You applied to a college you knew nothing about. You were fully aware of the fact that the only reason why you applied to this college is that you had a slim hope that maybe your crush/boss would visit you once a year during homecoming. To you, that once a year was reason enough. She wrote the letter of recommendation. You went to the interview in which you were asked odd questions you didn't understand the purpose of—such as, which three things would you bring with you to college in order to remember your past? Picture. Journal. What-the-fuck-ever.

You got in.

And it was at that college from which your crush had just graduated, the crush who led you there, that you met him. Instantly, he slips into your mind. Penetrates your thoughts. You don't know how or why, but he does. You resist being fully aware of this. You are most certain you are a lesbian. You have a gay pride tattoo. So there is no hope here. Even when he is your roommate for two years and you actively have to resist kissing him goodnight. Even when you have dreams about him that make your underwear sopping wet. Even then, there's the fact of a forever-a-lesbian with a big gay rainbow on your ankle going on. So yes, no hope here.

And yet.

The hope holds out for nine years. And then you have that Facebook conversation in which you type in those specific "I have a crush on you" confessional words, and then he dittos them, and then he takes a 26-hour bus ride to come see you, and then he slips himself inside you, and then you transition from being a lesbian to being a hasbian, and then five months later you are married to him. And you will stand on the wrong sides of each other during the ceremony because you are breaking tradition (and there will be no white dress but a cherry red cocktail dress and silver sparkling high heels and there will be no march down the aisle but a two-step down it with your mother), and your lesbian friends will be there to woot you on.

Yes. You are fully aware of the irony, of how if it weren't for your lesbianism, your crush on another woman, you would not have gone to that college, would not have met him, would not have felt this pleasure, this remedy to the sopping wet underwear, would not have finally admitted that you wanted to commit yourself to him for, well, forever.

So you are fully aware of the fact that the lesbians helped to deliver him to you.

And to that you slip off your sopping wet underwear, straddle the man you never thought you would allow yourself to straddle, and you say thank you, lesbians, thank you.

Sexcapade
Sex Fact 16

The human body, when deprived of gentle touch, experiences "skin hunger" which can lead to failure to thrive in infants and withering in elderly populations. Sex, especially in old age, can be a way to help keep skin nerve fibers active in consenting adults.

Condoms and Hot Tubs Don't Mix

Another Friday Night with Mr. Fun
by John King

What do you do when you come across a woman whose labia are oversized? Really big? Like butt cheeks?

If you're me, you treat her like a *princess*. That's why I'm Mr. Fun.

Orlando is crammed with adventure and misadventure. How could it not be, when I live here?

The girl with the gargantuan labia was Tina, but this story isn't about her because I enjoyed that delightful college junior last Friday, and Mr. Fun is about the future.

Mr. Fun is about now.

Mr. Fun works as a financial analyst for Daydream Workshop. I report to the Chief Accounting Officer there, not a creative, and the CFO insists with a despotic fervor that we must suitably represent the professional arm of the company. Brooks Brothers suits, Fitzgerald fit.

We have offices downtown, with our own sweet private parking lot.

At 5:45 P.M. on Friday I leave the office, I take my Toyota Camry, the Funmobile, to Wing House, for three Heinekens and some hot wings brought to me by some of Orlando's more gorgeous prancing specimens of femininity. They like me there. Big tipper, obviously. This will be fuel.

I swoop home long enough for some transcendental meditation to my L. Ron Hubbard music, whose instrumentals are really underrated. Fuck Scientology, incidentally. I need an hour or so to delve into myself, connect to the Everlasting Fun, or EF, and then to help Mr. Fun focus, a few lines of Ritalin off my big hardcover copy of *Atlas Shrugged*.

I tidy up the place, and here's the crucial part: I put on pristinely clean, 2,000-count red sheets, and the black satin comforter on my king-sized bed. 65% of women say they are more likely to sleep with a man because of clean sheets, and most sheets are not even in this league of clean sheets.

I put on a fresh shirt, slip my suit back on. Then--and this is how you know that I have truly *become* Mr. Fun- -I slide my size eleven feet into blue crocodile boots. Custom made. Reptiles from the Nile, straight from the Bible onto my tremendous extremities.

Crocodile hits the accelerator, and the Funmobile is on its way to only one place: the lounge at Colonial Lanes. Ten o'clock.

I know, I know.

But it's fucking classic. Everywhere the eye can see, mirrors proudly embossed with beer logos. Dangling lamps with little red shades over the bar that make the place look like some funky undersea anemone. Wood booths upholstered with eight different kinds of fabric.

Condoms and Hot Tubs Don't Mix

Karaoke Night.

My Brooks suit touches the bar, and there's a snifter of Hennessy waiting for me. I am going to need it to tolerate all these losers, hipsters, college kids who think they're being ironic, office slobs who think that they are having fun, except it's all so pathetic.

Some balding asshole in a short sleeve oxford shirt is singing "Don't Stop Believin.'" *You* should stop believing, you hapless prole.

The essence of karaoke is the falsity of our dreams aligning with the falsity of pop music, the desire for transcendence itself making transcendence im-fucking-possible.

Or almost impossible.

The problem is that you have to have a feel for pop music, know its clichés, and know which ones are hollowed out ("Don't Stop Believin'") and which ones can resonate through the listeners with a sense of ironic surprise throughout the crowd like a huge zen bell loud enough to make all the poon in the room start to get wet.

The one-armed deejay knows me, knows that I'm the big tipper, so when I slip him a C-note and my selections, I am on the stage in about ten minutes.

I start with "Let's Go" by The Cars, move to Duran Duran's "Union of the Snake," then close out my set with Journey's "Faithfully," partly out of spite to the "Don't Stop Believin'" cipher and partly to show these bitches how big my fucking heart is.

Journey is fabulous, man. Steve Perry is a *genius*. His phrasing and harmonies.

I can totally sing the *shit* out of these songs.

On my third tall Hennessy, I am feeling really good about myself, but the composition of the room is not favorable. I got big applause, but everyone is into their own scene. No one wants to let Mr. Fun into their hearts. Some nights are like that.

I am leaning against the bar, my blue crocodile boot grooving into the foot-railing. The poon on tap won't make eye contact, won't be swayed into my orbit. This is okay, though. Totally okay. Totally. Normally, some University of Central Florida girl would feel my wealth, my power, my fun, but I am a hunter-gatherer, and a hero's journey seldom goes smoothly.

I slap down a twenty, and make my triumph to the exit. Tina is there with a fella at a table by the door. She's biting her lip. I give her a smile and a wink. I wish the fella luck, which he'll need because he most certainly is *not* Mr. Fun.

A quarter past midnight finds me peeling open the scarred door to Whiskey Lou's. The stench of smoke is its usual shock. I am tempted to smoke out of self-defense, but Mr. Fun is going to need the full use of his lungs tonight. All of Orlando is counting on it.

Unlike the slow immersion at Colonial Lanes, I make a hasty survey and then plop onto a high-top bar stool next to a woman in a black, sheer dress, slumped shoulders, feet wobbling onto the footrests.

"What'll you have?" I ask.

"Mmmm?" she says.

"Fireball!" I proclaim, and the waitress knows what to do.

"I *am* Mr. Fun," I say, offering her my hand.

"Mmmmm?" she says.

"What's your name?"

"Cynthia."

Her eyes are blackened with make-up, and I see that she's not especially young, and that this night has not been kind to her, but I also see that she had beautiful round cheekbones, and I can see just how irresistible she must have looked when she was in college, and I almost want to take her camping. Cynthia is beautiful, Orlando, make no mistake about that.

I smile at Cynthia until I get her to smile back. Her breasts may be small and her auburn hair may be a little limp, but that smile, coherent or not, is blissful.

The waitress puts down two shots and gives us both a smile. She leaves me the bottle.

Knowing that the Fireball will need some alchemy, and needing some noise to cover over the smacking of billiard balls, I strut up to the Touch Tunes and play "All Summer Long" by Kid Rock. I strut back, which makes the patrons of Whiskey Lou's cheer, and back at the high-top Cynthia is drinking her cinnamon whiskey with a sour look on her face, and when she sees me her face is contorting, smiling with pinched eyes, like holding back tears.

"It can be a little strong," I say.

Cynthia squints at me, pours another shot, darts it into the back of her throat, then stares at me. This gets me so hard, but I hope it doesn't show, or make me seem ungallant, you know.

"I fucking hate Kid Rock," she said. "He spit on me at a show. I had front row tickets."

"Huh," I said. "He was lucky if you were in the front row, Cynthia. Truly fucking lucky. I don't have a high opinion of him, either. I just put this on because the machine doesn't have 'Sweet Home Alabama,' and you are so beautiful, Beautiful, that you remind me of 'Sweet Home Alabama.'"

Cynthia smiles so big it crests through her drunkenness. I pour us another round of Fireball. I can't wait to kiss her to taste the cinnamon. Cynthia is my liquor of choice.

We leave her Prius in the parking lot next to the beachside mural. I kiss her. I can sense the years of disappointment in all that sweetness. We head back to my place.

She's clacking around my hardwood floors on black pumps, and she seems uncertain of where to go, what to do.

I pour us more Fireball shots, which she gratefully swallows. I gaze into her eyes, which are struggling to focus. "You are so beautiful, Cynthia," I say.

I put Warren Zevon's "Excitable Boy" on my Bose Soundtouch 520 system. Cynthia has wobbled into the bedroom, is running her fingers over the plump black sheen of the comforter, and the magic sensation of the red sheets. She runs into my arms, her shoes flinging off her feet.

She's biting my neck flesh, and sort of crawling up me and slipping and crawling up again, and I grab her and knock her into my Gustav Klimt prints. Her eye makeup all smeary, her lipstick drifting across onto those round cheekbones, but her breath is making me hot, and I upend her onto the mattress where she bounces three times before coming to rest, and I reach between her legs and fumble for panties, which are some stretchy polyester things that are reluctant to slide down until she pushes off the mattress with her feet, and she is shuddering by the time I fling glittery gauze over my shoulder.

I slide my jacket off just before digging my head beneath her dress until I reach her crotch, and I jam my lips against hers, trying to imagine them by touch alone, sucking them and trying to make her feel like she is so beautiful, like she is driving me crazy, like she has completed this algebra of cosmic romantic psychosexual need of my soul, and my nose is mooshed against her clit and I am not going to stop yet because I don't need to breathe more than she needs to feel my tongue and when the Fireball and the darkness and the tang of her secretions seems to be interconnecting in some neural crossfire that tastes like ozone do I flop out from the sheer black fabric and gasp for life.

I can see her chest rising and falling rapidly, like her tits are doing some kind of aerobics. Cynthia turns her face away, turns over onto all fours. I stand there breathing deeply myself I rub her ass, which makes her rear back, and I really don't know what she is thinking. Gently, I lift the dress until its hem is across her back, and she does not respond, except to twitch when I trace my finger across her skin. I grab her beneath her armpits and slowly, but firmly lift her until her body is leaning back against mine. I fidget with a clasp at the back of this dress, but can't figure out its mysteries, so I reach around her waist and clutch her breasts, and her being half-clothed this way, with her hot skin scraping my cock made me feel oddly impassioned, yet tender.

I pinch her nipples through her bra for a long time, when eventually she reached her right hand behind herself and stroked me until I got fully hard, and then she tugged and tugged until she slithered between the bed and me.

Cynthia scrunched her dress over her hair, let it flop onto the wood, then unclipped her bra.

She ambles up onto the high plateau of my bed, on her hands and knees, her spine arching, her head lowered and curtained by her dark hair.

She is breathing in and out, but otherwise still--like a lamb patiently standing before the gate that will soon open onto a conveyor belt.

I watch her for a moment, pray that she won't puke up Fireballs all over the 2000-count sheets.

She murmurs, finally, "What are you waiting for?"

Cynthia's a pro.

I snap my fingers, which awakens the 237 LED candle-tip points in the ceiling and walls and some of the furniture.

I caress her plump, curvy ass while she seems to be mumbling something that might be a prayer.

Cynthia is so beautiful. I hurry off my shirt, and then bunch my pants and boxers down to my knees, atop my boots. Then I remember that my Trojan magnum is back in my pocket, so I yank the pocket inside out for it, and rip the foil and roll it on.

On the bed, I pull Cynthia close from behind. She smells like sweet fire. It takes about fifteen tries to get my cock angled enough to enter her because despite her warmth and wetness down there, she was despite her vintage very, very tight.

Her head hung low over the red sheets, and I could only faintly see her face. She was smiling. She was crying. Her eyes were so dark.

Her thighs ground into me.

In the floor length mirror flecked with dim spots of light, her smallish boobs jerked with each thrust, each nipple like a candle flame.

My impending orgasm was like an angel soaring uncertainly over the entire world, not sure which was land and which was void in the dark, but surging with undifferentiated electricity, the glory and beauty of this moment, this moment which might be the only moment to ever exist, and then there was a silhouette upon the Earth, this sudden catch of recognition, this nation to fly over so angrily, so sublimely, this place where the truth is revealed, this rediscovered country in the shape of Sylvia, my college sweetheart, this faithful touch that is everything I am not, that is a reason to face another day, to release it all, to yield it in this special place.

Cynthia was asleep by the time I returned from the bathroom.

•••

In the morning I gave her a fresh toothbrush. She was wise enough not to ask how many spare toothbrushes I own.

I took her to IHOP, and enjoyed the pleasure she took in devouring a thoroughly disgusting funnel cake. The comfort foods of beautiful women are one of the world's stranger mysteries. I, obviously, had the big steak omelette.

The I drove her back to Whiskey Lou's. I gave her a long sweet kiss and then let her retreat to her car and drive away.

Then I drove home, so the celestial rites of purification could begin.

Penis Cheese
by Heather Startup

It was a dark night in early November. I wore tight jeans and a sexy black top that my husband thinks is super hot. But I wasn't dressing for my husband, who wasn't even out with me that night. I was going to a sex party.

Okay, it wasn't a sex party. It was one of those parties where women sell shit to other women after everyone's gotten tipsy. Don't try to invite me to one of *those* parties if you're selling Tupperware. I'm not buying Tupperware and calling it a night out with the girls. Even if you're selling health supplements, just don't. Your sales rep will be all, "You all want to be healthier, right!?!" and I'll be the one who looks her dead in the eye and says no.

But maybe that's what the wine is for. After a couple glasses, my deadpan no will turn into a "Yes!!!" real fast—not that it will be sincere or lead to any pill sales. But I can accept an invitation to boozy get-togethers involving toys and lingerie.

Diane had invited me through Facebook, so I knew a few of our mutual friends would also be there. When I got to her house, I made a beeline for the kitchen, where the women clustered around the wine, crackers, and penis cheese.

(I should clarify. There was a soft cheese display that someone had shaped into a penis. At the time, it didn't occur to me that this might be considered gross—I love cheese and dove right in as soon as the penis cheese had been duly photographed and presumably Instagrammed).

But when I was offered chilled wine, I made the mistake of saying yes before finding out if there was any wine that had already been chilled. (The answer was no.) And when Diane stuck a bottle in the fridge, I said nothing, even though part of me felt like I really, really needed some wine, goddammit.

It wasn't the sex part that was making me neurotic. It was the party part. It was the gathering of confident, sassy women talking about sex. It was talking about sex in the obligatorily unabashed way that occurs in all-women gatherings when you've been friends for a few years. It was the expectation that, once those friendships have ripened, you will be more honest and vulnerable than you were when you first met.

It was knowing my friends were about to find out I was a bit more of a contrarian than I tried to be around them. My family once fled an Olive Garden in terrified embarrassment when my father and I got into a heated argument over corporate ethics. Their departure didn't worry me. I just kept arguing and eating my carbs. At a sex party, although you're certainly supposed to dive right into the pecker-ino, you're not supposed to argue. Beneath the veneer of liberation, the politeness of everyone doing the same thing holds sway.

Condoms and Hot Tubs Don't Mix

Still, I enjoyed chatting with the other guests before the party started. The attendees weren't only a handful of Diane's friends. Her college-age daughter, Julia, was there too. I knew I never would have gone to a Tupperware-esque sex party with my mom, even if she had been the host. The one time Mom ever talked to me about sex beyond "Don't do it until you're married," it involved a discourse on nipple play that made me wonder if opening the car door, jumping out, and hitting the pavement at forty-five miles an hour would really be that painful. Whatever Mom was up to was fine by me as long as she didn't tell me about it, and she never asked about my sex life, and we were both very happy that way, thank you very much.

Still, it was oddly comforting when Julia came into the kitchen and asked, "When's the sex party gonna start?"

"It's a Pure Romance party," Diane said. This exchange would repeat itself a few times throughout the evening, each woman sassily showing she was cool enough to talk about dildos with Mom/Daughter.

And the ethos of a sex (products) party for women is a veneer of no regrets—a veneer belied by the drinking and the intentional absence of men but, like a sheer teddy or lacy camisole, a fun outfit to try on even if you can't wear it everywhere.

The consultant's name was Shirley. While we'd poured each other glasses of wine and stuffed our faces with penis cheese, she had set up a table covered in dildos, vibrators, gels, and, of course, catalogs. We settled around her on sofas and chairs as Shirley introduced herself, then the products.

There was a dildo you could stick to any surface. There were lubes that tasted like fruit. There were vibrators we could turn on and pass around to feel the tips and ascertain that they were up to the job. And there were questions—lots of questions.

I hadn't prepared for this part of the party. My feeling of being caught off guard wasn't some sort of misplaced test anxiety that I was reliving from high school exams; it was, instead, about Shirley's rather interesting approach to knowledge. Shirley would ask us a question, and whoever shouted out the correct answer would get a raffle ticket. If you asked Shirley a question, you could also get a ticket. At the end of the evening, the winning ticket would earn you a prize. I was generally behind the eight ball whenever an activity required asking questions of and yelling out answers to a centralized authority figure. The yelling didn't seem orderly, and the groupthink it engendered gave me the creeps. Generally, when a person at the front of a room declares an answer to be correct or incorrect, I want to ask them for their peer-reviewed journal articles. (Again: contrarian.) Instead, I usually refrain, both from making this very reasonable request and giving any answers I might otherwise be inclined to shout out. A sample of bubble bath lasts an evening, but the self-respect that comes from refusing to yield to a questionable authority lasts a lifetime.

Condoms and Hot Tubs Don't Mix

Still, Shirley didn't look much like a cult leader. She looked more like a middle-aged woman who worked as a college administrator and sold sex products outside of her day job, which is what she was. And after a while, even though the wine was wearing off, I decided to try a little harder to trust that Shirley wasn't trying to brainwash me. By the time we got to the question, "True or false: only gay men like to be penetrated," I let out a resounding "No!" with the rest of the group. (I'm sure there's a story about how we all knew this and why we were so insistent on it. I'll ask around.)

Part of my motivation to join in was for the raffle. Hey, free stuff is free stuff. And you don't insult the lady who's invited to sell you sex toys by implicitly declaring that raffle prize isn't worth competing for. And you don't let your friends beat you in a sex-knowledge contest. As I warmed up, I answered more questions—but everyone else was amping up their response rate too.

Then Shirley told us it was time to draw penises. We would all be competing to see who could draw the "best" penis. "Best" was left undefined, leaving my peer-review-demanding side unsatisfied, but I was glad for something to do that wasn't a call and response with Shirley's sex prompts. And the twist made it even better: we had to draw the penises on our heads.

No, we weren't drawing on our faces with markers like you do to the first girl to fall asleep at the slumber party. We had to put our blank papers, attached to clipboards, on top of our heads and draw blindly.

It was the first thing all night that I had studied for.

•••

In high school, the only time I suspected I'd been given a pity A was in art class. This was really nobody's fault, least of all my instructor's. Mrs. Tome was an excellent teacher; she taught me aspects of drawing and painting that had never occurred to me, like shading and crosshatching and just the fact that there were pencils with differing amounts of darkness. And I tried—as much as I knew how. I'd never had to try in any other classes except PE, for which I never got a pity A because I almost always earned B's. Any A I got in PE was definitely for real. But getting an A in art, while certainly nothing to complain about, was truly perplexing. I looked at the masterpieces the students around me produced, glanced back at the scribbles I was desperately hiding under my crossed arms, and figured if there was a grading curve, half the class had flushed it down the toilet. But I kept trying.

One day, Mrs. Tome made us assemble a collection of objects on the tables in front of us. Then we had to draw them—without once looking at the paper. *Artists have to look at the thing they're drawing*, she explained, *not at the pencil marks they make. And you can't get comfortable with looking at the thing you're drawing until you learn to feel your way across the paper.* It was painstaking and miserable; at first, I ended up with something that might have been an abstract urban skyline if it were viewed generously. None of my lines connected from beginning to end, forming a coherent object.

But I kept trying. By the end of the lesson, I had drawn a serviceable representation of the collection of objects on my table. They weren't detailed, but they were recognizable. I could feel my way through the dark.

•••

With the clipboard balanced on my head, I began to draw. I had never thought of myself as being very proprioceptive. I'd taken a multiple-intelligence test in high school, and although I aced the nerd categories, the category measuring whether you can keep track of where your body parts are took a nosedive down to the seventeenth percentile, making me marvel at how I'd kept myself alive for seventeen years. Plus there were those B's in PE.

But now I knew I had Mrs. Tome on my side—not that I thought she would approve of my using skills from her art class to win a penis-drawing contest, but that didn't matter. What mattered was how my hand felt as it moved the pencil over the paper. It was familiar; I could almost see it. As everyone around me squinted or rolled their eyes upward, I put the finishing touches on my penis, hoping the little hairs on the balls weren't as misplaced as a tail pinned on the wall next to the donkey.

Shirley declared time was up, and we all took our penises off of our heads. Mine was just as I'd hoped:

a more or less closed shape clearly resembling a penis that any graffiti artist would have been proud to call their own. The head was appropriately mushroomed, the shaft was jauntily erect, the balls were correctly located at the base, and the hairs had all hit their target.

The other penises didn't fare so well. Half of them weren't closed shapes, even if you squinted. The other half were vague or malformed, resembling the now-half-eaten penis cheese more than they looked like an actual dick. My penis stood a chance.

Shirley asked Diane to judge and then had us line up our penises—unsigned to rule out bias—in the middle of the carpet. Diane peered closely at each one, ruling out the abstract-cityscape designs before settling on three to select from. Mine was one of the three. Diane went back and forth among them.

"This one's not the biggest," she said finally, pointing at mine, "but it is the most realistic." She held it up as the winner.

When I claimed the drawing, I had a faint twinge of doubt. Maybe I had imagined I'd drawn it. I couldn't possibly have won the penis contest, not with my contrary streak and my lack of proprioception. But no one objected. No one even looked surprised. Diane handed me my drawing, and Shirley handed me my prize.

The prize was either a bag of samples or a cupcake-scented body wash; I don't remember because shortly thereafter Shirley drew my name from the raffle. She looked rather nonplussed, either because I'd just won something or because I'd barely participated in her Q & A. Either way, I was the proud new owner of body wash, body oil, a shaving cream that allegedly doubles as hair conditioner, and some kind of magical strawberry-flavored cream that you're not actually supposed to eat.

Then again, I'm pretty sure you're not supposed to eat penis cheese.

Sexcapade Sex Fact 17

Humans are the only mammals with permanently enlarged breasts. Other mammals have full mammary tissue only while they are nursing.

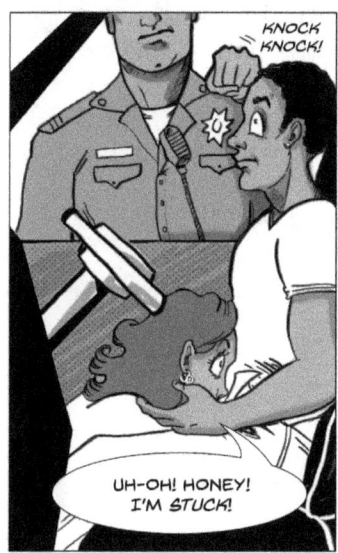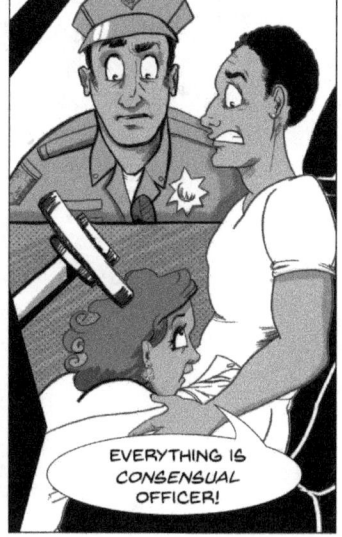

Coptus Interuptus *BABS! the great*

Sexcapade
Sex Fact 18

A single human egg or sperm's DNA is equivalent to about 37.5 megabytes of data. This means the data transfer in a single 2 to 5 milliliter ejaculation would be equivalent to 7,500 to 18,750 terabytes of data.

Ants
by Anusha VR

Two foodies shouldn't date
There must be a rule as such.
Especially not foodies
who are also alcoholics to boot.
After the eighth shot of tequila
the man you've been with since college
wants to spice things up.
And what better way
than a can of whipped cream?
Any idea is a good idea
when your veins are pumping
more liquor than blood.
Halfway through gorging on
scrumptious cream bandeau bikinis
the hooch works its magic.
We fall asleep wearing half eaten
whipped cream lingerie.
Take it from me,
it ain't half as fun
as the sitcoms portray it to be.
But if you still insist
on mixing food and sex,
Let me ask you a question
Do you want to get ants?
Because that's how you get ants.

Sexcapade
Sex Fact 19

Men giving themselves a coffee buzz will also give their little swimmers a buzz. The concentration of caffeine in the blood of men who have recently drank coffee is almost the same as the concentration of caffeine in those same men's semen.

Hard Workers
by Kate Rigby

I'm Bobbles. Bobs for short. I'm one of the workers. We all lie on the bed together, we six, in the quilted valley, wondering whose turn it'll be tonight. Pearl's, I expect.

Pearl's popular with our employer. A workaday sort with a healthy salmon colour and happy veins entwining her like ivy. Americans would say she's "kinda regular" and therein lies her attraction. She's got good proportions. Average height, slim but not skinny.

"It won't be me," I say, rolling into Shad. "Ms Locke doesn't like me. I think she wants to throw me out on my ear."

Shad nudges me. "I'll be hot on your heels, Bobs!"

Me and Shad, we stick together. Shad is Ms Locke's token black worker. If Ms Locke were black, who would be the token white I wonder? They tell me Ms Locke made a bee-line for Shad, paid good money for her but now she's gone off her. God knows why. Shad's kinda regular too. Like Pearl in black, only half an inch taller.

Goldie is to my other side. "You're a real mover, Bobs. You shake that body. You can do things for Ms Locke like none of us can."

"But she said I hurt her, Goldie."

"She needs to get used to you, that's all, Bobs. You are her newest recruit."

"Whereas Pearl's stood the test of time."

"Exactly. But I've been here a fair time, and I'm not all that hot with Ms Locke, you know," says Goldie. "Look at me. Aren't I a bit jaded?"

I'm looking at her. She's solid gold to me. A rock. "Take a good look, Bobs."

I look into her tall satiny eight-inch form, but all I get is my wonky face refracted back at me. I suppose she's got a point.

"Maybe it'll be my turn tonight," says Janet, voice soft as jelly. But you can see right through Janet with the gloopy face. And what you see is glitter glitter glitter. Did you ever see the like anyway? She's not *real*, that one. Mind you, I can talk, covered in all my bumps, looking like a walking disease. Who wants someone like me? It didn't take long for Ms Locke to pass judgement. She screamed at me last week. "Get out! Get out! You vicious bitch."

But at least I'm not starting to smell like Janet. It's that squishy skin of hers. There are traces, residues. Fluids dry all tacky on her and she doesn't scrub up clean.

Condoms and Hot Tubs Don't Mix

"None of us is secure," says Melody, and we all groan. If anyone is the favourite around here, it's Melody. And her such a dinky thing! Half the height of most of us and so slender. Such a small pointed head on her. But she can stand up for herself, can Melody.

"We must stick together," says Shad. (Melody turns up her nose at the thought of sticking to the reeking Janet.) "Fight for better conditions. What say the workers?"

"Better conditions?" says Pearl. "But it's such a cushy number here. Lounging around until she's ready for one of us."

"Ready for you, Pearl, don't you mean," says Shad. "It's not enough. I want work every night. I don't want to be no token black cunt."

We all laugh. "That's one thing you're most definitely not, Shad!"

But we can't complain. OK, so we don't get paid as such, and we can be called upon to perform any old time of day or night but it's live-in-all-found and we've been on some exciting journeys since we came here, we six. Even lumpy old me! We've shimmied through lush gardens on our way up to the cave, we've heard incredible animal sounds, it's what we came to do.

Shh! Shh! It's Ms Locke's girlfriend at the front door. With wine. Offering apologies for the other night. We hear the pop of cork, the *glug glug*, the chink of glasses. Now they're on the settee in reconciliation, hands in private places. But hang on a sec, they're rowing again, same as Saturday.

"No I'm not," shouts Ms Locke.

"Yes, you are," bawls her girlfriend.

"Oh screw you," shouts Ms Locke. "I'm going to let my hair down with Goldie."

We all look over at Goldie.

"Hard as nails that Goldie one," says the girlfriend. "Well, if you'd rather spend time with that lairy fat-so than me, then I'm off."

"You do that."

"Ah, I've had it anyway," says the girlfriend, "sharing you with all and sundry."

We hear the slam of the front door, and then the flitting of Ms Locke's footsteps up the stairs.

"Now then darlings," she says, lying back on the quilt with us. "Which is it to be? Pearl? Or Melody, my lady?" Her red-nailed hand takes hold of Melody. "I only said Goldie to wind *her* up."

Melody is a good little worker. She loves what she does. She, out of all of us, knows Ms Locke inside out. But even she cannot please Ms Locke tonight.

"You're useless, Melody. Crap! Not one of you has got any balls." Ms Locke is punching her pillow in frustration.

She's going to take it out on someone. Yep. She squeezes me and Shad in her right palm and suddenly we're flying through the air to pastures new. Well, to next door's moonlit swimming pool anyway. Splosh. Cor, Janet would have welcomed this - a midnight dip

Condoms and Hot Tubs Don't Mix

to cleanse that skanky body of hers, but it's us. Me and Shad. Floating on our backs. Strictly speaking, I'm not supposed to get wet, it might damage my innards, my ability to hum good, but who cares?

Because I'm in heaven, riding the waves with Shad; and when the temperature drops and we're starting to shiver, I say, "Shad, should we snuggle in together?"

"Ooo yeah," she says, as I squeeze my bobbles into her with sensual movements until we're stacked together as one.

The following morning, we slip apart, bobbing on the water, like buoys. Or should that be boys? We're almost boys, aren't we? We never did understand why we were saddled with such daft feminine names. Though Shad would probably say, "You speak for yourself, Bobs. I'm all girl."

Suddenly we're aware of little-girl feet dangling at the side of the pool, swishing, swashing, making waves. Then the swishing stops as, curious, she watches as we drift towards her. Before we know it, we are being trawled ashore in a fishing net and left on the concrete as the child goes indoors, flip splashy flop. "Cor, this is the life, Shad, eh? Sunbathing on the terrace. Better than next door."

When the child returns we're almost dry, except for our private bits. We thought we'd landed a right plum job here too, sun-lounging half the day, but the child's got other plans for us it would seem.

"Grandma," she calls. "Grandma, look what

I found! Sausages for my cook set! One is done black like Gramps has them and the other one is still raw!"

Grandma peers at us uneasily as though something about us rings a distant bell. "Oh yes," she says. "Funny shaped sausages though, dear."

Shad whispers into my ear, "That's it, Bobs. I'm ready for the chop."

First Published in The Diva Book of Short Stories (Ed: Helen Sandler), Diva 2002
Also Published by Pfoxmoor Publishing 2011

Condoms and Hot Tubs Don't Mix

Boy in the Bathroom
by Nina Robins

The day the boy took me
to the bathroom
my hair wasn't brushed like usual
and I checked my breath,
it was ok,
and we went into the boys dorm.
The one above the cafeteria.

This was going to be the first
kiss in a year
and we didn't know each other's names.

So I puckered up
and sat on the window sill
but he fell to the floor
and kissed my feet instead.

I didn't have time to apologize
for the athletes foot,
or the nylons,
but he stayed there five minutes

Nina Robins

just necking with my ankle

until staff knocked on the door,
and he yelled out
I'm taking a shit!
It's fine I'll be down to lunch in a minute,

using the excuse of watching
his feet under the door to
keep kissing mine.

My neck lonely
for this attention
just glancing out the window
at the snow outside.

We never spoke again
after that.
My friends would shout out
foot fetish! When he came around
but that's all.

I think his name was Joe.
I think I wouldn't have minded if he kissed me.
My feet weren't the ones who were lonely.

Even the boy I gave the bathroom to
only took what he wanted.

The Penis Fly Trap
by Anne Champion

Men who pose with cats on Tinder automatically get a right swipe from me. It's a difficult forum to mine for men who don't think of themselves as some sort of Tarzan, so I figure a man with a cat is secure in his manhood, and he might possibly even be nice. It's like those videos you see with gorillas petting kittens and doing sign language—miraculous.

Jan had a cat on his chest in his profile picture, and he even went a step further: his bio said "cat enthusiast." I had two cats that were more important than people to me, so I figured Jan would understand me in ways other men don't.

He checked off a few of my other essentials too: no guns in the pictures, no pictures of extreme sports, no dead fish, no pictures of a child with a bio that says "not my kid." He was practically ideal until I saw the photo of the car selfie.

I don't understand men and car selfies, but I want it to stop. I can almost understand the guns and the fish—it basically says look, I am man, I am hunter. But what is going on with the car selfies? I guess cars are a symbol of masculinity, but we can't even tell what kind of car it is. I don't know if you can drive fast or if you can zipzag through traffic seamlessly or if you're going anywhere cool. For as much as men mock women for their selfies, why do men sit in their car, strap on their seatbelt, and think, *yes, this is just right, let me take a selfie.*

But he was a "cat enthusiast." For some things, you make compromises.

We matched, and I sent the first message: "So, you love cats?"

He replied that he had a cat growing up, but it was with his family in Puerto Rico, but he loved it and missed it. I visited Puerto Rico once with a couple girlfriends after a bad break up. We did coke every night and got blackout drunk and made out with waiters, so perhaps Jan and I could connect about his homeland; I'd just have to water down the details a bit.

After a little chatting, I gave him my number, and Jan sent me selfies of him reading at Starbucks. No dick pics, no comments on my tits—Jan was looking like the Holy Grail. I sent his picture to my gay office mate from work, asking "What do you think of this one? Good?"

He replied, "Good enough."

It's true that Jan lacked sex appeal, opting instead for a kind of goofy bordering on nerdy charm, and his hairstyle looked different in every picture. In one it was parted down the middle and slicked to his head with gel. In another it was coiffed in a swoop over his head at least three inches high. In another it was messy and uncombed. Each one looked wrong, like Jan just hadn't found himself yet.

But I'm not vain—I was looking for some personality, some kindness, and a cat lover. It was also warm outside and I had a new dress. It was time to go on a date.

With Tinder, you have to strike when the iron is hot. I can't explain why, but if I talk to a man on Tinder for more than two days and we haven't met, my desire suddenly expires. So, when Jan asked me to meet him at a bar that night, I immediately jumped in the shower and set to the task of removing all my body hair.

Everything was perfect—Jan was cuter in person. He had a lovely smile and he laughed readily at all my jokes. He listened to stories about my cats, he loved *Game of Thrones*, and he was well versed on the Israeli Occupation and was sympathetic to the Palestinians. Jan looked more like boyfriend material with every cocktail.

After a few drinks, we got up to leave, and Jan offered me a ride home. It was clear from Jan's lack of flirtation that he'd be a "gentleman" and leave me with a hug, but I was determined to redirect our fate. When we got to my driveway, I said something I knew he couldn't resist.

"Wanna come upstairs and meet my cats?"

"I was really hoping you'd ask," he said.

And so Jan met my cats, who were conveniently snuggled on my bed, which gave us a reason to perch ourselves there with some wine. Soon, the wine was gone and Jan lay down. If I waited for him to make the first move, I'd be up all night and would be out a decent night's rest, which was becoming more and more out of the question in my thirties. So, I zeroed in on my target and I kissed him.

Everything changed once we kissed. Jan went from being near perfection to seeming like an inexperienced teenage boy. Once our lips touched, something wild ignited in him, and it was like watching a pack of hungry mice released into a maze in which there's a slice of cheese at the end. Every part of Jan's body interacted with mine in an unchoreographed and frenzied manner, bumbling and bumping and groping. He immediately climbed on top of me and started to furiously dry hump me, grabbing one of my breasts and repeatedly squeezing it like he was milking a goat. His tongue and my tongue couldn't seem to find a rhythm, mostly because his rhythm was too fast for me to follow, and he kept doing unexpected things like licking my teeth and leaving a snail trail of drool all over me in his wake.

Still, I was resolute. There's a lot I can forgive, and first time sex can be awkward. I thought we could hit a stride, but I had to tell him, "Slow down, Jan. Just enjoy it."

He seemed embarrassed and he slowed down for a few minutes, but his dry humping just got harder and harder. I was confused by its urgency—he was truly dry humping me as if he were deep inside of me and getting tremendous pleasure from it. I hadn't dry humped since I was thirteen, but I didn't remember it being so strenuous. I had to make it stop.

"Jan, let's fuck," I said.

"Okay." He dutifully began taking off his clothes.

I started to take off mine and I reached for a condom on my nightstand. I knew from the dry thrusts that there would be little foreplay: I had to let this eager puppy out of the storm and indoors soon.

When I turned over to face him, Jan was on his back fully nude, and that's when I saw it—Jan's penis, a two inch tall mushroom, barely visible in the unkempt shrubbery of his pubes.

Perhaps it wasn't hard? I reached for it—it was a fossilized little mushroom, standing at full attention. He moaned with pleasure.

Then I realized that Jan wasn't the perfect man at all. Jan was charity work.

Sex is charity work when you have sex with someone not out of desire, and not for your own pleasure, but because someone is a really nice person and deserves some pussy for being nice. It's a cold, cruel world when you're a single girl, and many men manage to objectify you or degrade you even when they're just breathing, so a man like Jan must be rewarded.

I'd had sex with small penises before, but never as small as Jan's, and never with someone as clumsy and eager as Jan, so I just knew it wasn't going to be good.

I handed him the condom, "You do it," I said. I was too embarrassed to try to put it on myself, and I figured he'd have to have some kind of tricks to make it fit.

He seemed to get it on without any problem because he was slobbering on my face in no time. I wasn't even sure if we were having sex or not, but I didn't want to ask him if it was in. After a few thrusts, I felt as if someone were fingering me with the tip of a thumb, and Jan was unleashing some porn star status panting and moaning, so I knew my charitable contribution had been met.

After Jan came, he pulled out and looked down. "Oh," he looked confused, "Where's the condom?"

"What? What do you mean?"

"It must have fallen off," he said, tilting his head, squinting, and peering between my legs like a dark cave.

I felt between my legs. Nothing. He started to look around on the bed. Naked and scrambling, his tiny penis seemed to mock me.

"Do your cats eat condoms?" he asked. In fact, one of my cats did have an affinity for the taste of sex soaked latex, and he'd eaten them and pooped them out in the past.

"But you never left my vagina!" I protested, "How could my cats get the condom?"

"I don't know. Unless it's inside of you."

I bolted for the bathroom and squatted over the toilet and peed, hoping it would fall out on its own. Nothing. I felt around the outside of my vagina for any trace of rubber I could yank out. Nothing.

Now I have to admit one of my deepest secrets: I have an extreme phobia of vaginas. Plunging my hands inside of myself is simply unfathomable to me. I haven't even masturbated without the barrier of a vibrator between myself and my vagina.

I can't tell you why I'm afraid of my vagina. I'm sure I have a perfectly pretty snatch, and I should get to know it better. But once, as a teenager, I saw someone on TV say that every woman should regularly use a hand mirror and get to know herself. Not one to pass up sex advice, I got a hand mirror, sat on my floor, spread my legs, and looked—and was utterly horrified. It was as if someone had cut open my stomach and showed me my intestines. I couldn't begin to make sense of what was going on down there, and the next day I went to the local Planned Parenthood and asked the gynecologist to tell me if it looked normal.

"Have you had any symptoms that you need to tell me about?"

"I don't know," I said.

"What do you mean you don't know?"

"I mean, I've had sex before but I used condoms, but I looked at it the other day and I don't know if I have weird growths down there or something," I said.

She took one look at it and diagnosed it as a *beautiful, perfectly healthy* vagina.

I trusted her, but I have spent my whole life avoiding touching or looking at it.

So, this was a particularly revolting conundrum for me. I needed to fish around inside myself, but I couldn't bear how that would feel. I tentatively put my index finger inside myself up to my first knuckle, and I dry heaved. I don't understand why people like the way that mush of flesh feels.

I put on a robe, went to my closet in my room, and found a pair of winter gloves. "Did you find it?" Jan asked.

"No," I said, taking the gloves and retreating back to the bathroom.

Once I had the gloves on, I was able to plunge into myself with the same disgust that I felt taking a scalpel to a pig's lung in 8th grade. Even though I was able to get a couple fingers inside me (not without some serious clenching resistance from my body), I couldn't feel a thing with the gloves on. It was useless. I went back to the bedroom.

"I know we just met and I know this is awkward, but I'm going to need you to search for it."

"I have been searching! I've looked all over your room!" he said.

"Inside of me."

"Oh," he said.

"I'm sorry. I can't find it and I just need you to go up there and look for it. Dig around a little."

"Ok," he said. He really was an upstanding guy.

I lay down and readied myself into the position of a gynecological exam. Jan put his head between my legs and put several fingers way up inside me. He really put in a valiant effort, but he came up with nothing. Not a trace of it.

"I bet I can find it with my penis?" he said. I looked at his crotch and marveled at the fact that somehow Jan had managed to be turned on by this pelvic exam. I was worried about the condom, but it's not as if Jan's little penis could jam it up inside me any farther, and I couldn't get to Planned Parenthood to have it removed until the morning. So I gave him another condom, and we fucked again.

But this time, before he finished, Jan stopped. "Um, it happened again."

"You lost another one?"

He pulled out. "Yep, it's gone."

"Oh my God, Jan! I'm not a trash can! You can't just leave your garbage inside of me!"

We went through another ordeal of searching and came up empty handed. I decided it was time for bed.

"Can I sleep here?" Jan asked.

"No, I'm sorry."

"Really?" I guess most women let men spend the night. But the one thing I still had to look forward to in this night was a good night's rest where I could toss and turn and snore freely, unbothered by how I looked in the morning. I'm not a fan of men spending the night, and I felt especially fatigued by the knowledge that I'd be sleeping with plastic wedged somewhere inside my body.

"Keep me posted on the condoms," he said, as I walked him to his car.

The next morning, I woke up early and went straight to Planned Parenthood. I'd never had this problem before, so I felt monumentally ashamed to have to vocalize it to someone. However, I consoled myself with the thought that doctors and nurses work with human bodies, and they've certainly seen much worse, because bodies do some straight up nasty things.

I got there, went through the metal detectors, and went straight to the front counter.

"Do you have any walk in appointments?"

"What kind of appointment do you need?" she asked.

She was going to make me say it. Right here, out in the open, in front of a waiting room of people. I leaned in and lowered my voice.

"Well, this is really embarrassing, but I think I have a condom inside of me."

"Okay, well, we don't have anything available until Tuesday." It was Sunday. She didn't seem to understand the urgency.

"Actually, I have two condoms inside of me," I said.

She didn't flinch. She was completely unfazed. "Well, if you think it's a medical emergency, you can certainly go to the ER," she said.

"I mean, am I ok? Will it get infected? Will I get toxic shock syndrome?"

"Generally condoms have a way of working themselves out of the body within a day or two," she said. "It would have to be there for a long time to get toxic shock, and you'd have symptoms before then like a really high fever, so you'd know."

"So, this is ok?" I said, "I mean, this happens to people? It's okay for me to wait until Tuesday?"

"Trust me," she said, "We've seen much worse things than condoms stuck inside people."

Like what? I wanted to ask—she'd unexpectedly piqued my curiosity. My friend Moe's father was a rectal surgeon, and while he mostly seemed to operate on things like cancer, she'd written stories about him having to dislodge things like Frodo action figurines from a man's anus who said he was dusting while naked and fell on it. I suppose people who don't have body phobias get much more creative than I do.

I made an appointment for Tuesday, but while I waited, I couldn't help but be supremely uncomfortable with the knowledge that I had condoms inside of me. I tried to think back on what I knew about my basic sexual anatomy: I knew I had a vaginal cavity that was *supposedly* only a few inches deep, a cervix, a uterus, ovaries, fallopian tubes, and all that jazz, but *where* exactly were these condoms? Were they shoved up inside my cervix? Did they travel through my fallopian tubes? Was I literally pregnant with two condoms? My body felt like a deep space with no light, and somewhere, two condoms traced a constellation of my shame.

It turns out both condoms were hiding behind my cervix. The doctor reassured me that everything was okay, nothing was infected, and I had nothing to be embarrassed about.

"If it were infected, you'd know—you could tell by the smell," she said. This fact just exponentially increased my vagina phobia.

I texted Jan that the condoms had been successfully excavated from my body. My charity work was done. I went back to Tinder.

Less than a week later, I met Solomon. Solomon was *truly* perfection: he was more than just a nice guy or a cat enthusiast. He was a PhD student at Harvard studying Middle Eastern history with a focus on the Ottoman Empire. He'd gotten his undergrad in classic literature at Oxford, and was born and raised in London, though his parents were of Indian descent. He had an accent, he had charm and charisma, he had lively intelligent conversations, he quoted the first lines of Jane Austen novels, and he was a feminist. I'd truly struck gold.

Though when I first met Solomon, my initial impression was that he might be hiding something, like the fact that he wasn't sexually interested in women. There was something so delicate about his mannerisms, something so pristine about his collared shirts and neatly pressed khaki shorts and black rimmed glasses. He later told me that he is frequently mistaken for homosexual, and he's regularly hit on by men. "It's because I'm *European*," he explained. That somewhat convinced me, until I asked him his celebrity crush on one of our first dates, and he answered, without hesitation, Prince.

It was befuddling, but this was *the man of my dreams,* and a little homosexuality or bisexuality has never been a barrier to love for me. After our first date, which was seven hours of lying in the grass in the Boston Public Gardens, I called my friend and reported, "I want to marry him."

So I was determined that our second date would end in sex. I invited him to a bar down the street from my house. After a couple drinks, I invited him to my house. After more drinks, he kissed me on my couch. His lips were perfect, his kissing was perfect, everything was perfect, and so I blurted, "I want to have sex with you."

"I want to too," he said. And I took him to my room.

He was tender, passionate, attentive, and generous—and then he got naked. Solomon, like Jan, had a very small, very thin penis. Solomon may have had a couple inches on Jan, but he still made me worried about the lack of snugness of the condom.

I know I sound like a superficial size queen, but the truth is that I didn't care about Solomon's tiny penis—I knew Solomon was going to be good with it. He was too attentive to not be concerned about my pleasure. The problem was that I only had Magnums or regular Trojans. I'd never in my life even seen small condoms for sale, and this wasn't a regular occurrence, so I was unprepared. I told myself that what happened with Jan was a fluke, and I gave Solomon a regular condom.

To this day, Solomon is one of the best lovers I've ever had. We were in sync with each other, and I was thoroughly immersed in him when he said,

"God, you feel so good. You're *so* wet."

I stopped, "How can you feel that I'm wet?"

He pulled out of me, "Oh my!" he said, sounding so proper and British, "I don't know where the condom is. I think it fell off inside of you."

It was undeniable now: my vagina was a penis fly trap. In reading mythology, I'd come across the folk tale of vagina teeth. Myths of beautiful, irresistible women whose vaginas were actually mouths containing sharp teeth that would castrate a penis. The myths were meant to discourage rape or sex with an unknown woman, and I secretly loved the myth, because I'd love to Lorena Bobbit some of the assholes I'd had sex with, but now I was having sex with *nice* men, and my vagina turned on me, sprouting teeth and snatching off condoms left and right. My vagina was a monster. My cervix was an abyss where condoms got lost and held hostage.

"This has never happened to me before," he said. This made me feel worse. I wanted to know that this problem was a regular occurrence for small cocked men. I wanted this to not be the fault of my own powerful suction.

"Me either!" I said. I couldn't tell him this happened to me a week ago. This was the *man of my dreams*.

But I also couldn't go back to Planned Parenthood: it was too humiliating. I called my sister the next day.

"Well," she said, "you just have to give birth to it."

"How?"

"Get in a position like you're having a baby and fucking push!"

And so I did. I did it in the shower. My vagina phobia anxiety was still going strong and I felt like if I gave birth with hot water running over me, it'd be more relaxing. I also figured that if I had to dig, I could put a condom on over my hands instead of gloves so that I could feel it better. I knew this was risky—my penis fly trap might just suck the condom right off my hand like a vacuum cleaner—but it was my only solution.

So with a Magnum over my thumb and two fingers and my shower running, I laid down in the tub in the position to give birth: legs spread wide and arms gripping the sides of the tub. And I fucking pushed. I fucking pushed with all the strength I had. I fucking pushed until I was panting just like the women on TV who give birth. I fucking pushed until I was cursing Solomon for putting this godforsaken thing in me. I fucking pushed until I felt a tiny piece of rubber crest the surface of my vagina, and with my condom covered fingers, I yanked the thing out of my body.

It was all stretched out and misshapen—who knows what kind of arduous journey it went through inside my body? But I had the same instinct that one has when one births a bloated, red mess of a baby: I took a picture of it and sent it to all my friends.

"I did it! I birthed the condom!" They replied with relief and congrats.

Sadly, much like how babies don't cement relationships, the condom incident didn't bring Solomon and me closer as a couple. It didn't bring us to coupledom at all. Solomon wanted to continue sleeping with me, but I couldn't address the topic of small condoms, so we agreed to get STD tested and had sex exclusively, which means we didn't use condoms. (Remember, this was the *man of my dreams)*.

I probably held on to that delusion that many girls cling to: if I fucked Solomon enough, I could fuck him right into falling in love. My vagina is clearly powerful, after all, and he must have gotten many whiffs of my drunk with love pheromones. But unfortunately, that chemical imbalance caused by love never happened with him; I remained much more impressed with his charms than he was with mine. He still wanted to fuck me, but he never asked for anything else. The practical part of me says this is because he traveled a lot doing very important research for Harvard in the Middle East and he just couldn't put me through that. But the other part of me (Realistic? Paranoid?) thinks he's kind of like a purebred Persian cat—he's not supposed to mate with an ordinary mutt, but he will fuck one if it's in heat.

Condoms and Hot Tubs Don't Mix

The moral of the story is that you can carry condoms in your uterus for men and they show no gratitude for your sacrifice and no respect for your pussy strength; they won't even be appreciative that you were still down for them even though their dicks were small. So, either just stay home with your own cats rather than look for cat lovers on Tinder or stock up on some tiny condoms.

Sexcapade
Sex Fact 20

Popular wisdom has it that double bagging — using more than one condom at a time — may cause condom breakage.

However, scientific studies demonstrate that double bagging significantly reduced the risk of condom breakage from 1.8 percent to 0.2 percent.

Bios

Jennie Jarvis (Co-Editor): Jennie Jarvis is an award-winning author and screenwriter. Her textbook *Crafting the Character Arc: A Practical Guide to Character Creation and Development* is used by creating writing programs around the world. She has appeared in *Writer's Digest Magazine* and *The Florida Writer*, and she teaches writing at Full Sail University. She received her MFA in Creative Writing from Queens University of Charlotte.

Leslie Salas (Co-Editor): Leslie Salas holds an MFA in Creative Writing from the University of Central Florida and is a graduate of the University of Denver Publishing Institute. By day, she helps students in higher education master the art of effective communication and storytelling at an entertainment, media, and arts university. On nights and weekends, she writes in multiple genres, including poetry, prose, screenwriting, and comics. She is the editor of the anthology *Other Orlandos* (Burrow Press, 2017) and serves as graphic nonfiction editor for *Sweet: A Literary Confection*. Her work has appeared in *The Southeast Review*, *SmokeLong Quarterly*, *Rogue Agent*, and more.

Bios

BABS! the great (Illustrator/Comic): BABS! the great is a cartoonist, illustrator and graphic artist. BABS has published independent comics and as an illustrator for children's books. BABS received her BA in Visual Arts from Fayetteville State University in Graphic Fine Arts. BABS has a wide interest in sequential art, illustration and cartooning. Her current art mediums are pencil, ink, watercolor and digital mixed media. She currently works as graphic artist in beautiful downtown Vero Beach, Florida and is a freelance illustrator and comic book artist. Her website is www.BABSthegreat.com or find her on Tumblr: babsthegreat.tumblr.com.

Matt Peters (Publisher and Author): Matt Peters has an MFA in Creative Writing from the University of New Orleans and a BA in English from the University of Central Florida. His fiction and non-fiction have been published sporadically in various literary journals, culture rags, web zines, and anthologies over the last two decades. He teaches Publishing & Distribution in the Creative Writing Program at Full Sail University, and captains Beating Windward Press. Matt can be reached at MattP@BeatingWindward.com.

Contributor Bios

Stacey Balkun: Stacey Balkun is the author of *Eppur Si Muove, Jackalope-Girl Learns to Speak* & *Lost City Museum*. Along with Catherine Moore, she is co-editor of *Fiolet & Wing: An Anthology of Domestic Fabulist Poetry*. A Finalist for the 2016 Event Horizon Science Poetry Competition as well as the Center for Women Writer's 2016 Rita Dove Award, her work has appeared in *Crab Orchard Review, Gargoyle, Muzzle, Bayou,* and others. Chapbook Series Editor for Sundress Publications, Stacey holds an MFA from Fresno State and teaches poetry online at The Poetry Barn.

Catherine Carson: Catherine Carson's poetry and creative nonfiction have been published in *Gravel, Referentials Magazine*, the anthology *My Other Ex: Women's True Stories of Leaving and Losing Friends*, and the chapbook *There Will Be Xmas*. Her work has also been featured on the podcast The Drunken Odyssey. She holds an MFA from the University of Central Florida and teaches in Winter Park, Florida. She also serves as Poetry Editor for Burrow Press's *Fantastic Floridas*. Her best advice for a good night's sleep? Never spend a night without your CPAP.

Alex Celine: Alex Celine is a native of Orlando, Florida. She graduated with her bachelors in English from Stetson University and graduated with her MFA in creative writing from The University of Memphis. This will be her first publication. Alex is currently working as a teacher.

Anne Champion: Anne Champion is the author of *Reluctant Mistress* (Gold Wake Press, 2013), *The Good Girl is Always a Ghost* (Black Lawrence Press, 2018), and *The Dark Length Home* (Noctuary Press, 2017). Her poems have appeared in *Verse Daily, Prairie Schooner, Salamander, Epiphany Magazine, The Pinch, The Greensboro Review, Thrush Poetry Journal, New South*, and elsewhere. She was an 2009 Academy of American Poet's Prize recipient, a Barbara Deming Memorial grant recipient, a 2015 Best of the Net winner, and a Pushcart Prize nominee. She holds degrees in Behavioral Psychology and Creative Writing from Western Michigan University and an MFA in Poetry from Emerson College. She currently teaches writing and literature at Wheelock College in Boston, MA.

Chelsea Clammer: Chelsey Clammer is the author of *BodyHome* and winner of the 2015 Red Hen Press Nonfiction Manuscript Award for her essay collection, *Circadian* (October 2017). She has been published in *The Rumpus, Hobart, McSweeney's Internet Tendency, The Normal School* and *Black Warrior Review* among others.

She is the Essays Editor for *The Nervous Breakdown* and teaches creative writing online with WOW! Women on Writing. Chelsey received her MFA from Rainier Writing Workshop.

Gemma Cooper-Novack: Gemma Cooper-Novack's debut poetry collection *We Might As Well Be Underwater* was published by Unsolicited Press in 2017. Her poetry and fiction have appeared in more than twenty journals and been nominated for multiple Pushcart Prizes and a Best of the Net Award. Her plays have been produced in Chicago, Boston, and New York. Gemma was a runner-up for the 2016 James Jones First Novel Fellowship; she has been awarded artist's residencies from Catalonia to Virginia and a grant from the Barbara Deming Fund. She diablogs on sinnerscreek.com. Gemma is a doctoral student in Literacy Education at Syracuse University.

Christina Crall-Reed: Struck by lightning at the age of twelve and again as an adult, author/artist/humorist, Christina Crall-Reed lived on a Wisconsin dairy farm, in a house zapped by lightning more than twenty times. Today she lives in a metal-framed house, in the lightning capitol of the USA (Tampa, FL) - because she can.

In addition to creative pursuits, Christina worked in child abuse prevention, taught mural painting, was design director at a new age magazine, and is a Certified Laughter Leader through the World Laughter Tour.

Writing about the absurdities of life, lightning, and the healing power of laughter, Christina's Amish Crack House Series, (including the upcoming Pet My Pretty Lizard; Maybe Spinach Doesn't Like You Either; and her own coming-of-middle-age story, The Incontinental Divide) launched in 2017.

Timothy DeLizza: Timothy DeLizza was raised in Brooklyn, New York. He currently lives in Washington, DC, where he works as an energy attorney for the government. His first novella, *Jerry (from Accounting)*, is available through Amazon.com.

Bethany DuVall: Bethany DuVall writes fiction and personal essays. She has an MFA in creative writing, and has published over 60 articles on art, writing, and education. Along with these shorter works, she is pecking away at revisions on her novels. In 2012, Bethany teamed up with HD Counseling, LLC, to offer creativity workshops. That same year, she also founded the Shine Street Writers, which continues to foster Central Florida writers of all genres. Bethany teaches English at Full Sail University. She is the mom of a teenaged musician, is married to a man who knows every line of every '80's movie ever made, and is the servant herder of two cats. As someone who is pro-life, Bethany is proud to be part of a collection supporting Planned Parenthood, an organization that has dramatically reduced the demand for abortion in the US by providing education, contraceptives, and empowerment to women and families.

Holly Elliott: Holly Elliott has a doctorate in Creative Writing from Florida State University and has taught composition and creative writing at several colleges. She is currently a professor at Valencia College in Orlando Florida. Her work has been published in such places as *Strange Horizons, Dream Fantasy International*, and the anthology *Barnyard Horror*.

Cecilia M. Fernandez: Cecilia M. Fernandez is the author of *Leaving Little Havana: A Memoir of Miami's Cuban Ghetto*, winner of an International Latino Book Awards, and a finalist in the Bread Loaf Writers' Conference Book Contest. She is Emmy nominated, and her work has appeared in *Latina Magazine, Accent Miami, Upstairs at the Duroc: the Paris Workshop Journal, Vista Magazine, Le Siecle de George Sand,* and *Day One, A Literary Journal.* Cecilia earned an MFA in Creative Writing from Florida International University and an MA in English Literature from the University of Miami. Her undergraduate degree in journalism is from the University of California-Berkeley. She lives in Weston, Florida and teaches writing and literature at Broward College and Nova University. Currently, she is working on a collection of short stories, *Grieving for Guava*, among four other projects.

Peter M. Gordon: Peter M. Gordon's poems have appeared in *Slipstream, The Marjorie Kinnan Rawlings Journal of Florida Literature, 34th Parallel, The SandHill Review*, and *Poetry Breakfast*, among other anthologies and websites. Peter is past President of Orlando Area Poets, a chapter of the Florida State Poets Association. Peter's first collection of poetry, *Two Car Garage*, was published in 2012 by CHB Media. His latest, *Let's Play Two: Poems About Baseball*, was published in 2016. He has over 35 years' experience creating content ranging from live theater to digital video for media companies including HBO, PBS, NBC, and Golf Channel. Peter contributed articles to over 14 baseball history books, and his journalism has appeared in outlets ranging from *The NY Daily News* to the *West Orange Times*. He earned a BA from Yale and an MFA from Carnegie-Mellon, and teaches Business of Film in Full Sail University's Film Production MFA program.

John King: John King is the host of *The Drunken Odyssey: A Podcast About the Writing Life*. His work has appeared in *Gargoyle, The Newer York, Painted Bride Quarterly, Bachelor Pad Magazine,* and others. In 2010, he earned an MFA from New York University.

G.B. Lindsey: G. B. Lindsey's first love has always been writing: as a child, she cultivated such diverse goals as becoming "a cowgirl and a writer" or "a paleontologist and a writer." Her contemporary romance *One Door*

Closes is part of the *Secrets of Neverwood Anthology*, runner up for the 2014 Rainbow Awards. She loves to write sci-fi, romance, and historical fiction, and has a proud and salacious affair with the horror genre. Other hobbies include playing the piano, reading voraciously, the occasional period drama movie night, and devouring scary films for dessert. She completed her degree in Literature and Creative Writing from UC Santa Cruz, and more recently, her Master of Arts in Creative Writing in Newcastle, England. She now lives in California with her fluffy cat.

Steve Meador: Steve Meador has had three books of poetry published and when he is not on a photographic road trip you can find him in Florida writing or working as a real estate broker. His work has appeared regularly in print or online journals, resulting in numerous nominations for awards. However, he has yet to see his name at the top of the list. He is too humble to provide a long list of his publications, so, by the grace of God and the good work (evidently) of Al Gore, you can Google Steve and he will magically appear in the Internet search results.

Leah Mueller: Leah Mueller is a writer from Tacoma, Washington. She is the author of two chapbooks, *Queen of Dorksville* (Crisis Chronicles Press) and *Poilitical Apnea* (Locofo Chaps), and two full-length books, *Allergic to Everything* (Writing Knights Press) and *The Underside of the Snake* (Red Ferret Press). Her work has been published in *Blunderbuss, Sadie Girl Press, Origins Journal, Talking Soup, Silver Birch Press, Cultured Vultures*, and many other publications. She is a regular contributor to *Quail Bell* magazine, and was a featured poet at the 2015 New York Poetry Festival. Leah was also a runner-up in the 2012 Wergle Flomp Humor Poetry contest.

Kate Rigby: Kate Rigby was born near Liverpool and now lives in Devon, England. She's been writing for nearly forty years, with a few small successes. She realized her unhip credentials were mounting so she wrote *Little Guide to Unhip*, first published in 2010 and updated since. However, she's not completely unhip. Her punk novel, *Fall Of The Flamingo Circus* was published by Allison & Busby (1990) and by Villard (American hardback 1990). Skrev Press published her novels *Seaview Terrace* (2003) *Sucka!*(2004) and *Break Point* (2006) and other shorter work of hers. *Thalidomide Kid* was published by Bewrite Books (2007). She has had other short stories published and shortlisted. She also received a Southern Arts bursary for her novel *Where A Shadow Played* (now re-Kindled as *Did You Whisper Back?*).

Nina Robins: Nina Belen Robins is a three-time national slam poet and author of the books of poems "A Bed With My Name on It" and Supermarket Diaries". She lives with her boyfriend and cats and works in the bakery department of a supermarket. Her life goals are normalizing mental illness and living childfree.

Lisa Lanser Rose: Lisa Lanser Rose is the author of the memoir *For the Love of a Dog* (Harmony Books) and the novel, *Body Sharers* (Rutgers University Press), which was a finalist for the PEN/Hemingway Foundation Award for Best First Novel. Her publications and honors include the The Briar Cliff Review Nonfiction Award, The Florida Review Editor's Award, and a Best American Essay Notable Essay. She fosters herding dogs, trains trick dogs, and blogs with awesome women at TheGloriaSirens.com.

Jim Ross: After retiring in early 2015 from a career in public health research, Jim Ross jumped back into creative pursuits to resuscitate his long-neglected right brain. Since then, he's published over 50 pieces of nonfiction, several poems, and over 180 photos in more than 60 journals in North America, Europe, and Asia. His publications include *1966, Bombay Gin, Columbia Journal, Friends Journal, Gravel, Ilanot Review, Lunch Ticket, MAKE, Meat For Tea, Stoneboat, The Atlantic, and Thin Air*. His work was recorded in podcasts for *Drunken Odyssey, Friends Journal,* and others. One of his pieces contributed prominently to an upcoming major documentary film. Jim and his wife--parents of two health professionals and grandparents of four toddlers--split their time between MD and WV.

Joseph Sheldon: Joseph Sheldon *rears* himself for life's *ending* moments by keeping a healthy regime of booty squats. Besides discovering himself, he writes text based adventure games and illustrates for money, a job that doesn't keep up well when backed into a corner. He earned his Bachelor's in Creative Writing and has been published once before in the February 2017 edition of *Down in the Dirt*. He would call this *ass-inine*, but that would be the butt of the joke.

Heather Startup: Heather Startup is a Central Florida writer with an MFA from Queens University of Charlotte and several short-story publications under her belt. In addition to writing and attending ersatz sex parties, she enjoys hanging out with her husband, meeting other writers, and smashing the patriarchy. "Penis Cheese" is her first creative nonfiction publication under her own name.

Jameson Tabard: Jameson Tabard is a novelist and playwright from Orlando, FL. He holds a BA and MA in English and is currently a professor at a media arts university in Florida He studied and performed Shakespeare at Shakespeare's Globe Theater in London, where he learned that Renaissance theater was just an excuse for queens to dress like queens. Jameson has an unhealthy appreciation of the male physique, antiquated pop culture, and architectural relics. His novel *The Scottish Bitch* is available in print or e-book from Beating Windward Press.

Anusha VR: Anusha VR is a Chartered Accountant and Company Secretary residing in India. Her works have been published in over thirty anthologies. She is currently working on her chapbook slated for publication in December 2017.

Missy Wilkinson: Missy Wilkinson is a journalist and novelist living in New Orleans' Bywater neighborhood. Her bylines have appeared in *The New Orleans Advocate, Gambit Weekly, Huffington Post, Thrillist, xoJane, The Bitter Southerner, Jackson Free Press* and many other outlets. A small press published one of her novels in 2015 and collapsed shortly thereafter, but correlation is not causation. A Baton Rouge native, Missy has an MFA in fiction from the University of New Orleans and was nominated for a Pushcart in 2004. She is happily retired from stripping, but she hasn't forgotten how to walk in those crazy platform shoes.

Awkward Sex Fact End Notes

1. Maines, R. (1999). The technology of orgasm: "Hysteria," the vibrator, and women's sexual satisfaction. Baltimore, MD: Johns Hopkins University Press.

2. Lloyd, E. (2006). The case of the female orgasm: Bias in the science of evolution. Cambridge, MA: Harvard University Press.

3. Galinsky. A. (2012). Sexual touching and difficulties with sexual arousal and orgasm among U.S. older adults. Archives of Sexual Behavior, 41(4), 875-890.

4. Semans, A. & Winks, C. (2004). Sexy mamas: Keeping your sex life alive while raising kids. Novato, CA: New World Library.

5. Cooper, T.G., Noonan, E., von Eckardstein, S., Auger, J., Gordon Baker, H.W., Behre, H.M., ... Vogelsong, K.M. (2010). World Health Organization reference values for human semen characteristics. Human Reproduction Update, 16(3), 231-245.

6. Truesdale, M.D., Osterberg, E.C., Gaither, T.W., Awad, M.A., Elmer-DeWitt, M.A., Sutcliffe, S., ... Breyer, B.N. (2017). Prevalence of pubic hair grooming–related injuries and identification of high-risk individuals in the United States. JAMA Dermatol, 153(11), 1114–1121. doi:10.1001/jamadermatol.2017.2815

7. Puppo, V., & Puppo, G. (2016). Comprehensive review of the anatomy and physiology of male ejaculation: Premature ejaculation is not a disease. Clinical Anatomy, 29(1), 111–119.

8. Wright, P.J. (2013). U.S. males and pornography, 1973-2010: Consumption, predictors, correlates. Journal of Sex Research, 50(1), 60-71. doi: 10.1080/00224499.2011.628132.

9. Ogas, O. & S. Gaddam. (2012). A billion wicked thoughts: What the internet tells us about sex and relationships. New York City, NY: Plume.

10. Yoshie, N., Nakao, A., Ishimaru, E., Terashima, M., Yamada, T., & Kotani, J. (2014). Unusual rectal foreign bodies: A case report and review of published works. Acute Medicine & Surgery, 1(1), 61. doi: 10.1002/ams2.9

11. Bijlani, R.L., Vempati, R.P., Yadav, R.K., Ray, R.B., Gupta, V., Sharma, R., ... Mahapatra, S.C. (2005). A brief but comprehensive lifestyle education program based on yoga reduces risk factors for cardiovascular

disease and diabetes mellitus. Journal of Alternative and Complementary Medicine, 11(2), 267-274.

Brotto, L.A., Mehak, L., & Kit, C. (2009). Yoga and sexual functioning: A review. Journal of Sex & Marital Therapy, 35(5), 378-390.

Dhikav, V., Karmarkar, G., Verma, M., Gupta, R., Gupta, S,Mittal, D., & Anand, K. (2010). Yoga in male sexual functioning: A non-comparative pilot study. Journal of Sexual Medicine, 7(10), 3460-3466. doi: 10.1111/j.1743-6109.2010.01930.x

12. Apodyoposis. (n.d.). In Urban Dictionary online. Retrieved from https://www.urbandictionary.com/define.php?term=apodyopsis.

Gymnophoria. (n.d.). In Urban Dictionary online. Retrieved from https://www.urbandictionary.com/define.php?term=gymnophoria.

13. Herbenick, D. (2009). Because it feels good: A woman's guide to sexual pleasure and satisfaction. Emmaus, PA: Rodale Books.

14. Herbenick, D. (2009). Because it feels good: A woman's guide to sexual pleasure and satisfaction. Emmaus, PA: Rodale Books.

15. Sgobba, C. (2015). What really happens when you fracture your penis. Retrieved from https://www.menshealth.com/health/what-is-a-penile-fracture

Awkward Sex Fact End Notes

16. Sehlstedt, I. Ignell, H., Backlund Wasling, H., Ackerley, R., Olausson, H., & Croy, I. (2016). Gentle touch perception across the lifespan. Psychology and Aging, 31(2), 176-184.

17. Jahme, C. (2010). Breast size: a human anomaly. Retrieved from https://www.theguardian.com/science/2010/may/14/breast-size-evolution

18. Lindermann, C. (n.d.) Dr. Lindemann's Fun Sperm Facts! Retrieved from http://www2.oakland.edu/biology/lindemann/spermfacts.htm.

19. Beach, C.A., Bianchine, J.R., & Gerber, N. (1984). The excretion of caffeine in the semen of men: Pharmacokinetics and comparison of the concentrations in blood and semen. J Clin Pharmacol, 24(2-3), 120-126.

20. Planned Parenthood Federation of America. (2011, July). Fact sheet: The truth about condoms. Retrieved from PlannedParenthood.org.

Acknowledgements

This anthology wouldn't be possible without the generosity of all of our amazing authors and our illustrator/comic artist, all of whom agreed to have their work published without payment. This unselfish donation of their creative work allows us to donate the proceeds of this book to Planned Parenthood, an organization that has been working to provide sexual education and birth control services for over 100 years, and we can't imagine being able to publish an anthology about awkward sexual encounters without their existence in this country.

We would also like to thank the amazing staff and interns at Beating Windward Press, for their hard work and dedication to the production of this book - Jayde Reid, Amanda Cuevas, Victoria Leeworthy, & Kathleen Parker. These thanks go out especially to Matt Peters who put up with our nagging.

On a personal level, Leslie and Jennie would also like to thank their partners - Jesse and Phil - for the continued support and excellent sexual encounters that led to them having the cutest babies in the world - Vincent and James. In addition, we would like to thank the literary community of Central Florida for providing us with the opportunity to not only meet each other, but to grow as literary creators as well.

www.ingramcontent.com/pod-product-compliance
Lightning Source LLC
Chambersburg PA
CBHW051538020426
42333CB00016B/1985